To my daughter, Alison, and my husband, Gordon

## Joan Mowat

P·C·P

Paul Chapman
Publishing

Paul Chapman Publishing
A SAGE Publications Company
1 Oliver's Yard
55 City Road
London EC1Y 1SP

SAGE Publications Inc
2455 Teller Road
Thousand Oaks, California 91320

SAGE Publications India Pvt Ltd
B 1/I 1 Mohan Cooperative Industrial Area
Mathura Road
New Delhi 110 044

SAGE Publications Asia-Pacific Pte Ltd
33 Pekin Street #02-01
Far East Square
Singapore 048763

**Library of Congress Control Number: 2007927002**

**British Library Cataloguing in Publication Data**

A catalogue record for this book is available from the
British Library

ISBN 978-1-4129-2914-1
ISBN 978-1-4129-2915-8 (pbk)

Typeset by C&M Digitals (P) Ltd, Chennai, India
Printed in Great Britain by the Cromwell Press, Trowbridge, Wiltshire.
Printed on paper from sustainable resources

# CONTENTS

# CONTENTS OF THE CD ROM

**Chapter 1**

Initial organization checklist

Pupil referral form (1)

Pupil referral form (2)

Permission letter to parents

Pupil permission slip

**Chapter 2**

Long-term target (example)

Target-setting template

Pupil Support Booklet/Card (Primary and Secondary)

Support Group Diary

Parents' leaflet

**Chapter 6**

Area of Concern Form

Support Group Pledge

**Chapter 7**

Programme of activities

Pupil folio checklist

Support Group Leaders' Guide to Activities

Support Group Leaders' Reflective Diary

Parent report

**Pupil Activities**

■ Index

■ Information sheets (x9)

■ Introductory section

■ Section 1

■ Section 2

■ Section 3

■ Section 4

■ Plenary section

**Support Group Evaluation**

Support Group Evaluation Checklist

Evaluation Tools

■ Class teachers' questionnaire

■ Parent questionnaire

■ Pupils' interview

■ Pupils' self-assessment checklist

  • pre-intervention

  • post-intervention

**Chapter 8**

Evaluation template 1

Evaluation template 2

Evaluation criteria

Support Group processes affecting stakeholders

**INSET materials**

Presentation for School Staff (Primary)

Presentation for School Staff (Secondary)

Presentation for Support Group Leaders

Presentation for Parents

# HOW TO USE THE ACCOMPANYING CD ROM

Throughout the book, you will see this CD icon used. This indicates that there is electronic material available on the accompanying CD Rom. Whilst reference may be made to individual materials on the CD Rom within several chapters of the book, the materials on the CD Rom have been placed in relation to the most relevant chapters.

All the materials and guidance needed to carry out the Support Group programme of activities are contained in pdf files on the CD Rom. You will need Acrobat Reader version 3 or higher to view and print these pages. The document is set to print at A4 but you can enlarge them to A3 by increasing the output percentage using the page set-up settings for your printer.

The CD Rom contains writable pdf files with checklists and pro formas for use in implementing a Support Group programme.

There are also four PowerPoint presentations, which may be run in association with a Support Group programme by the purchaser/user of this book within their own institution.

# About the Author

Joan, a practising teacher for twenty-eight years, commenced her teaching career as a Music Teacher in a Secondary school. Having been involved in voluntary organisations working with children and young people and having worked as a Care Assistant in a Children's Home, Joan developed her interest in the welfare of pupils over the course of her career. She taught in a range of schools encompassing those in leafy suburbs, inner-city schools and areas of significant deprivation. Joan has had responsibility (over a seventeen-year period) for two Music departments and, latterly, held the position of Depute Head Teacher.

Joan undertook a range of post-graduate qualifications, including the Scottish Qualification for Headship and is currently completing a Ph D at Glasgow University – 'Teaching for Understanding: within the Affective Field', based upon an evaluation of the Support Groups. She was the joint recipient of the SCRE Practitioner Award in 1997, drawing upon her work in promoting positive behaviour (see p. 105). She undertook a short-term secondment for the Scottish Executive, working as a National Development Officer for the project, 'Better Behaviour – Better Learning', taking forward pupil participation and peer support in Scottish schools.

Joan is keen to take forward consultancy work with Local Authorities and schools. She is currently a lecturer in Educational and Professional Studies at Strathclyde University and can be contacted at joan.mowat@strath.ac.uk.

For further information on the research study and its findings, please refer to the Conference Paper which was presented at the ECER Conference in Geneva in 2006 which can be accessed at www.leeds.ac.uk/educol/documents/157588.pdf.

# ACKNOWLEDGEMENTS

I would like to thank the Gordon Cook Foundation for their support; Bob Gibson, former colleague and mentor; Stuart Hall from the Scottish Council of Research in Education; Professor Eric Wilkinson at Glasgow University; Professor David Perkins for his encouragement; and all staff (teaching and non-teaching), pupils and parents at the school who made the development of the approach and conduct of the research possible, in particular the Support Group Leaders, who did a sterling job.

# PREFACE

'It wasnae only me' is an expression that will resonate with teachers throughout the land. As a newly appointed Assistant Head Teacher of a Secondary school in a deprived area of the West of Scotland, I became aware of the sense of despair I felt when the same pupils were referred to me for indiscipline day after day. Nothing that I did seemed to make any difference. I found many parents to be equally despairing, some of them, despite social work intervention, struggling to maintain parental control. Whilst the school had a Pupil Behaviour Support Base to which pupils with behavioural difficulties could be sent by classroom teachers if it was felt that they were not coping within the classroom situation, in reality, many pupils were abusing the system and deliberately misbehaving in order to be sent to the Support Base. Clearly a different approach was needed.

After discussion with the Senior Management Team and Behaviour Support staff, and with the involvement of a social worker (for the first year), it was decided to establish Behaviour Support Groups for the year group for which I was responsible – 13- to 14-year-olds (Year 9/S2) in the hope of reaching out to young people, enhancing their life chances and the life chances of the pupils who shared classrooms with them.

What followed was an intense period of contemplation as I set out to devise the approach during which I drew on my personal experience as a teacher of 20 years, my experience as a mother (what would I want for my own daughter?), the previous research and development work which I had undertaken into Promoting Positive Behaviour (Mowat, 1997) and the interest I had developed in the work of David Perkins and Howard Gardner of the Harvard Graduate School of Education. Whilst there are many approaches to working with children who are perceived as having Social and Emotional Behavioural Difficulties (SEBD) and which rely upon the development of social and communication skills, emotional literacy, anger management techniques and/or positive thinking, I believe that, valuable as these approaches are, they are not sufficient in themselves. It is only through reaching a deep understanding of who we are as individuals and how we relate to others and through encouraging children to develop an awareness of their innermost thoughts and feelings that we can seek to develop the long-term values and beliefs which will guide their lives and which will help them not only to understand their rights, but their responsibilities towards others.

This is no easy undertaking, but with a team effort and with access to a carefully and thoughtfully prepared programme of activities, it can be done. In the seven years over which the programme has run within the school, 150 pupils have participated within Support Groups, 16 members of staff have volunteered to lead groups in addition to the author, and the work of the groups has been thoroughly evaluated within an action research study focusing upon the progress of the first four cohorts of pupils to participate within Support Groups – 69 pupils in total. More in-depth accounts were obtained from six individual case studies of Support Group pupils, their parents, Support Group Leaders and class teachers, undertaken by the author in collaboration with Stuart Hall of the Scottish Council for Research in Education.

The book presents the approach itself, an opportunity to 'meet' some of the pupils through short case studies and a brief outline of the research study and its findings within the context of recent developments in education.

## A brief overview of the book

The principal aim of this book is to provide the necessary information and material such that the approach can be implemented within a range of educational settings. The approach should be applicable to pupils within mainstream and special schools in Upper Primary and Lower/Middle Secondary stages and can be implemented by any caring adults who take the time to familiarise themselves with the materials and the underlying philosophy.

The initial chapters set the scene, giving an overview of the types of approaches adopted within Support Group work and advise upon how Support Groups can be set up and managed. The aims and underlying theories of the approach are explored in Chapters 3 and 4.

It is also important to understand where this initiative resides in relation to national priorities for education, the quest for social inclusion and equality, and national drives to improve educational standards and school discipline. This is the focus of Chapter 5. Chapter 6 advises Support Group Leaders about how to teach for understanding and how to create an appropriate climate within the group. Chapter 7 introduces and gives examples of the pupil materials, the guide for implementation and means of assessing pupil progress.

Many initiatives fail not because they are basically unsound, but because they have failed to engage the 'hearts and minds' of all concerned. It is important therefore to ensure that change is managed effectively and efficiently at whole-school level and is sustainable – the focus of the penultimate chapter. The final chapter draws from the findings of the research study to illuminate the factors that are likely to make a difference in terms of pupil outcome and to look to the wider implications of Support Groups.

## Overview

**An Introduction to Support Groups: What Are They and What Is Their Function?**

Chapter 1    An introduction to Support Groups: planning and setting up a Support Group

Chapter 2    The Support Group in action

Chapter 3    The aims of the approach

**The Context of Support Group Work**

**Implementing the Approach**

**The Wider Picture**

# AN INTRODUCTION TO SUPPORT GROUPS: WHAT ARE THEY AND WHAT IS THEIR FUNCTION?

# An Introduction to Support Groups

This chapter describes:

➤ the constitution of the group: when, how often and where it meets
➤ the staffing of groups
➤ the criteria for and means of selecting pupils for Support Groups
➤ the management implications at the initial stage of setting up groups

## The constitution of the group: when, how often and where it meets

Support Groups consist of three to six pupils led by one or more adults, who meet regularly for a portion of the year (normally for the equivalent of a school period – 55 minutes each week) to undertake a series of activities that promote reflection and understanding. The groups may vary in size depending upon a range of factors – such as the degree to which the pupils present difficulties or the criteria by which pupils are allocated to Support Group Leaders, the optimum size being four. Larger groups, whilst appearing to be attractive in resource terms, do not provide the opportunity for the deep probing and personal attention which are the hallmarks of the approach and may also present difficulties in management, given that the target population is that of pupils with SEBD (Social and Emotional Behavioural Difficulties). All of the groups that have operated within the studied school have been same-age groups, but it should be possible to operate groups that combine two year groups. The danger in expanding beyond two year groups could be that the emotional maturity of the pupils would vary too widely to lead to meaningful discussion.

When, where and how frequently groups meet will be very much at the discretion of the individual school and the available resources. Within the school, the decision was made that groups should meet during the timetabled school day, after appropriate negotiation with class teachers and the school timetabler, in order to maximise attendance at groups. The first period of the day was generally avoided as many of the pupils likely to be placed in groups had problems with punctuality; times in the school day when pupils were more likely to be restless (just before lunch, the end of the school day) were likewise avoided. One of the strongest findings to emerge from the study was that Support Group Leaders recommended that groups should meet twice weekly in order to maximise the impact of the initiative and to re-inforce what was being taught such that pupils could apply it effectively in their day-to-day experiences of school.

Whilst it is often the case that interventions for young people tend to be of a generally short duration, relying on a high impact approach, when one is seeking to develop understanding that will ultimately lead to changes in behaviour, this is not appropriate. Some pupils are resistant initially and others, whilst being willing to co-operate, have difficulty in changing established ways of thinking and behaving, as is reflected in this comment from a pupil talking to a Support Group Leader (SGL):

> SG pupil: *It took time. I used to muck around with friends and that – not any more.*
> SGL: *Why's that?*
> SG pupil: *Because I've just come to my senses – this year's important for me to study for my exams.*

If adopting an approach of one session per week, the ideal provision to aim for is 20 sessions, commencing perhaps eight to ten weeks into the school year, enabling pupils, at the end of the year, to 'stand on their own feet' and to try to put into practice what they have learned. If pupils were to meet twice weekly, the sessions could be delivered either in a single block of ten weeks or in two blocks of five weeks with an intervening period during which pupils could still be monitored.

When considering appropriate accommodation, account needs to be taken of the likely needs of the group. Ideally, a small room should be sought with a central table around which pupils and their Support Group Leader(s) can work, with access to an outreach area. The room chosen should reflect the ambience of the group – informal but disciplined – and should be situated away from distractions.

## The staffing of groups

The majority of staff who volunteered to lead groups were Pastoral Care teachers or Behaviour Support staff. However, following an invitation to staff to observe a group in action and the provision of in-service training (see Chapter 8), a number of staff who became involved were class teachers with no additional pastoral responsibilities. Special Needs Auxiliaries attended groups if the pupils for whom they were responsible were involved in the initiative and senior pupils also offered their services.

In the opinion of one of the senior pupils, this was of mutual benefit to himself and the pupils within the group:

> *As the group progressed, the pupils began to enjoy attending, so as to use the group as somewhere they could talk freely about their experiences and problems … I was impressed by the improvement in the group.*

One of the teachers who afforded herself of the opportunity to observe a group, stated:

> *on my visit, the group were discussing very relevant issues, such as bullying, fighting and peer pressure.*

Whilst many senior managers in schools, who are ultimately the last link in the discipline chain, might be concerned about becoming involved in leading groups because of the danger of role conflict and of compromising their authority, I can only speak from experience in stating that it was one of the most rewarding aspects of what is a very difficult and demanding job. The pastoral role of senior manager has a dual function in that not only is one responsible for maintaining discipline, one also has a prime responsibility for pupil welfare.

This is paralleled, in some schools, by the role played by Pastoral Care/Guidance/Form teachers in fulfilling a supportive role for pupils whilst also guiding them in relation to discipline matters. Balancing these two aspects of the role whilst trying to meet the needs of pupils, parents and staff is a very tricky (and at times, almost impossible) feat. If one is to effect improvement in pupils, whether in terms of behaviour, work attitude or quality of work, the imperative is to win trust. No amount of haranguing or punishing pupils will have any effect if pupils are not prepared to listen and to give consideration to what is said to them and it is the establishment of respectful and trusting relationships which lies at the heart of promoting positive behaviour and effective school discipline. There are no quick, easy fixes!

This sentiment is expressed eloquently in the two quotes below, the first from a highly respected senior pupil who had worked with me voluntarily as a classroom assistant supporting pupils with behavioural difficulties (in relation to a previous research project – Mowat, 1997) and the second from one of the first pupils to become involved in Support Groups and with whom I discussed the potential conflict between my role as Support Group Leader and disciplinarian:

*And what can you do? [teachers] – you can shout at someone, you can give them a punishment exercise, you can send them for someone else to shout at them, you can give them a holiday. And the majority of pupils when they get to that stage won't care and their parents won't care either. It would be ideal if it [good behaviour] could come from within and I think it could … but, even if it doesn't, you have to find some other way of doing it, and although punishment has a place, on its own, it's going to do nothing. (Senior pupil)*

SG pupil:   *I used to worry that you would pass on what I was saying to my Mum and others but you didn't.*
Author:   *Did my joint role of discipline/welfare help or not?*
SG pupil:   *Yes, it helped a lot. You listened to my version of things when I was in trouble and that made me listen to what you said.*

Support Group work provides the ideal context in which to develop trusting and respectful relationships as pupils and teachers gradually begin to perceive the more positive aspects of each other. The means by which this can be achieved is discussed more fully in Chapter 6 and is reflected in these statements below:

*He [Mr L] made us feel welcome. He wanted us to have a good education and achieve something with our lives. (SG pupil)*

*It was very satisfying personally. I was able to get closer to the students. (Mr L)*

Indeed, the gradual development of trust between adults and Support Group pupils extended, for some pupils, beyond this relationship to other teaching staff and even to family relationships.

*[group work] helped my relationship with my Mum and Dad [never used to talk to my Mum]. Then I started the group and she used to ask me how I was getting on and I started to talk to her. (SG pupil)*

Perhaps one of the most important considerations in deciding upon who is best placed to lead a group is to give consideration not to the status or role of the individual but to look at the personality and characteristics of the person. Support Group work requires patience, strength, perseverance, compassion, someone who has unerring faith in human nature, intelligence, a sense of humour (absolutely essential!), a willingness to listen, to learn and to be open to new ideas and a firm but fair approach.

It is essential that all staff who are new to the approach go through a period of induction in which they are provided with a high degree of support. The means by which this is achieved is discussed in Chapters 2 and 8.

---

**Reflection Point**

Concerns about indiscipline in school are very much to the fore, as are concerns about a lack of respect in society generally. Do you agree with the comments of the senior pupil and of the need for trustful, respectful relationships? Do you feel that practice and policy within your school are conducive to the fostering of trustful and respectful relationships within the school community?

---

## The criteria for and means of selecting pupils for Support Groups

Resource implications apart, the most important criterion in the selection of pupils for Support Groups is to be clear about the purposes of the group and to ensure that the criteria used for the selection of pupils match these aims. Support Group work as described in this book is aimed towards pupils who fall within the following categories:

- those who are already exhibiting characteristics of pupils with SEBD

- those who are regarded by their class teachers and/or by teachers who have pastoral care responsibility for them as being at risk of developing SEBD.

However, what is meant by social, emotional and behavioural difficulties? It is very difficult to find a concise definition of the above as it covers a wide range of conditions, including those children classified as having Attention Deficit Hyperactivity Disorder (ADHD); those with externalising disorders (aggressive behaviour directed towards people and property classified as 'oppositional defiant disorder' and 'conduct disorder') and internalising disorders (anxiety and depressive conditions). In addition, children on the autistic spectrum may also exhibit aggressive behaviour arising from the distress they experience in coping with school life.

A definition within the report *Alternatives to School Exclusion* states:

> The term 'social and behavioural difficulties' is commonly used to describe the range of difficulties experienced by pupils who, for a variety of reasons, have not adjusted well to school or to living in the community. These difficulties vary in severity and frequency. The term includes those pupils who have persistent problems in responding appropriately to the disciplinary demands of school and whose disruptive behaviour places them at risk of being excluded. (SEED, 2001a: 6)

This is a common sense rather than a clinical view of SEBD which is helpful to educators and would be likely to accord with the views of practising teachers. The use of the word 'persistent' is significant in that it is the frequency with which pupils present challenging behaviour which is the issue in defining the target group of pupils who might be regarded as experiencing SEBD. It is a definition that would encompass a very wide spectrum of social, emotional and behavioural difficulties.

Working with the above definition, pupils who would be eligible for participation within Support Groups are those who are having difficulty in coping with the norms of classroom behaviour (and in the environs of the school) or those who are beginning to show signs of disengagement from learning, for example, persistent lateness, failure to bring equipment to school, failure to complete homework, in receipt of punishment exercises/detentions and excluded from classrooms for short periods of time. This will include a very wide spectrum of pupils, some of whom may be on the 'fringes' of going off-track, and others who have recognised disorders and may have been referred to psychological services. Indeed, many of the pupils who participated within Support Groups were referred to them through the Joint Assessment Team (JAT), a multi-disciplinary team of professionals which meets weekly representing social work, health, community and psychological services and school staff (professionals and para-professionals such as Home–School Link workers).

The number of groups a school can offer will depend on a range of factors such as the resources the school is able and willing to devote to the endeavour, which is largely in terms of staffing ('where there is a will there is a way' is a very important maxim in this respect), the willingness of staff to become involved and the number of children perceived to be likely to benefit from intervention.

Within the Primary sector, it is evident that the class teacher is the person who knows the pupil most intimately and therefore should be the person, in consultation with senior management and parents, who should be responsible for the nomination of pupils to Support Groups. Two approaches were adopted in the recruitment of pupils for involvement in Support Groups. The first was an invitation to Pastoral Care teachers to nominate to myself those pupils whom they felt would benefit from the approach using a pro-forma (see CD Rom) requesting information about:

- the reasons for the referral

- what the Pastoral Care teacher hoped the pupil would gain from participation.

The second, in an attempt to understand more fully the reasons for nomination within the Support Groups, was a questionnaire (see p. 8) derived and adapted from the definitions of Defiant Oppositional Disorder and Conduct Disorder.

Responses for the 36 pupils for whom referral forms were completed by Pastoral Care teachers revealed that the most prevalent behaviours were:

- defies teachers and/or refuses to obey rules

- argues with teachers

- deliberately does things to annoy other pupils

- blames others for his/her own mistakes

- loses temper

- is angry, resentful, spiteful or vindictive

- is touchy or easily annoyed.

## Support Group Referral

Please nominate any pupil for whom you think involvement in Support Groups would be beneficial. Pupils may be nominated for the following reasons:

- they are already having difficulty in meeting the norms of appropriate behaviour within the school environment.

- they are showing early signs of disaffection with learning and are 'at risk' of developing social, emotional and behavioural difficulties.

Please give some indication as to the reason for the referral by ticking the appropriate columns below and adding any other relevant information.

Pupil:                                                                     Class:

|  | rarely | sometimes | frequently |
|---|---|---|---|
| loses temper |  |  |  |
| argues with teachers |  |  |  |
| defies teachers and/or refuses to obey rules |  |  |  |
| deliberately does things to annoy other people |  |  |  |
| blames others for his/her own mistakes |  |  |  |
| is touchy or easily annoyed by others |  |  |  |
| is angry, resentful, spiteful or vindictive |  |  |  |
| swears or uses obscene language |  |  |  |
| truanting |  |  |  |
| stealing |  |  |  |
| physical fights |  |  |  |
| aggression towards others |  |  |  |
| ....................................... (other) |  |  |  |
| ....................................... (other) |  |  |  |

*Signature of referring teacher:*                                    *Date:*

Please return to:

The comments made by Pastoral Care teachers in support of the referral for pupils related to the potential benefits for pupils; concerns about a lack of application to classwork; the lack of co-operation/responsiveness to current attempts to support the pupil; family circumstances and the inappropriate nature of the pupil's behaviour. It is clear that the reasons for referral are many and varied and, for some pupils, the Support Group represents only one of the interventions taking place in their lives, representing a range of different services such as health services and social work, to tackle the complexity of the difficulties faced. This testifies to the need for a multi-disciplinary approach.

The information derived from these questionnaires was then used to plan provision for the session, deciding upon the number of groups to be offered in negotiation with senior management and Pastoral Care/Guidance teachers. The number of groups varied widely from year to year from one group of five pupils in one session to eight groups, catering for a total of 34 pupils, in another session but places were found for all pupils who required them. In allocating pupils to groups the following criteria were used:

- Pupils who were already under the auspices of the Behaviour Support Base were placed together in a group run by staff from the base.

- Pupils, where possible, were placed with their Pastoral Care/Guidance teachers.

- Pupils whose Pastoral Care teachers were not involved were placed either with myself, with staff who did not have a pastoral role within the school, or were slotted into groups where places were available.

- Account was taken of likely group dynamics. Exceptions were made to the above if it was felt that the constitution of the group would be likely to be discordant.

Parents were then approached informally by myself, Pastoral Care or Behaviour Support staff to broach the possibility of their children being involved in the Support Groups. Parents were also asked at this stage to raise the issue with their children, as did Pastoral Care and Behaviour Support  staff. After this initial approach, formal letters of permission were sent home (see CD Rom) and an invitation issued to parents to attend an information event held during the school day at  which they would have the opportunity to hear a short presentation (see CD Rom), meet some of the Support Group Leaders and raise any issues or concerns they might have about the participation of their children.

Whilst there were some pupils who were initially uncertain and, in a small number of cases, hostile to the idea of being involved within the groups, the majority of pupils seemed quite happy to be involved, some were clearly relieved to be offered help and support and there were occasions when pupils who had not been nominated requested to be included. In the case of those who were uncertain or hostile, they were informed that they had the option to withdraw from the group if they felt that it was not working for them. In the seven years of operating groups, only one parent refused to let her son participate (on the basis that previous attempts to help him in Primary school had failed); only one pupil failed to join a group after agreeing to participate; and only one pupil withdrew from a group after participating for a short period of time.

# Setting up groups: practical considerations

The most important criterion is for one person with real commitment towards the welfare of pupils with SEBD and towards the principles that underlie the Support Group approach to take on the role of Project Leader. It is imperative that this should be a whole-school approach if it is to succeed and it is advisable that the person concerned should either be a member of the Senior Management Team or someone who is able to liaise closely with senior management and has the respect of staff, parents and pupils.

The roles and responsibilities of the Project Leader at the initial stages would be to:

■ Liaise initially with senior management to agree in principle that the initiative can take place within the session and negotiate potential accommodation, staffing and resource needs (one copy of the book per Support Group Leader; photocopying; folders and box files) and the timetable which the group(s) might provisionally follow subject to negotiation.

■ Agree with senior management the processes that will be followed in relation to communication with the wider school staff, parents and pupils. All pupils and their parents within the class/year group should be informed of the initiative and its purposes if it is to gain acceptance within the school with the opportunity provided for them to raise issues and ask questions.

■ Gather a team of people who are likely to be sympathetic towards the approach and may potentially wish to become involved. Provide some initial in-service training to explain, in general terms, the aims of the approach using the materials provided (see CD Rom). Don't be too ambitious at the earlier stages.

■ Decide the class(es)/year group(s) you would wish to target and the people who will be responsible for nominating pupils.

■ Decide upon who will be involved in choosing pupils and allocating pupils to groups.

■ Put into place the procedures for the nomination of pupils and, on the basis of the returns, decide, using the mechanisms described above, upon the number and constitution of the groups matching this to the availability of staffing and accommodation. In the early stages, it is advisable to start on a small scale (one or two groups) and to build up thereafter if there is a need to do so.

■ Liaise once again with the Senior Management Team to communicate your needs and, if necessary, to re-negotiate the terms under which the approach will operate.

■ Decide finally, in negotiation with senior management, upon the team of staff with whom you will deliver the approach and set up an initial meeting for them to keep them involved in all stages of the development of the approach.

■ Put in place the communication systems to involve parents and pupils and organise the information session for parents (see Sample Letter and Information Booklet on CD Rom).

■ Arrange to have all necessary materials photocopied and distributed.

- When permission slips are returned (generally after some prompting!), decide, in negotiation with your team (Support Group Leaders), the location and timing of their groups at a time when you are also available to support them.

- Liaise with the individual members of staff (and their line managers) from whose classes pupils will be extracted for Support Group work and negotiate this with them on an individual basis. If problems arise, it may be necessary to reconsider and adapt the original arrangements.

- Inform all staff, the pupils (and their parents) in writing of the arrangements that have been made. Provide each pupil with a slip to show to their class teacher the first time they attend the group (see CD Rom).

A checklist the Project Leader can use to aid initial organisation of the groups can be found on the CD Rom.

**Summary**

This chapter has described the nature of Support Groups and provided advice about how they can be set up and managed in the initial stages. A whole-school approach with high quality communication is essential. The gaining of trust and of respectful relationships underpins the work of the initiative.

# CHAPTER 2

# The Support Group in Action

This chapter serves as an introduction to the approaches that are adopted in relation to Support Group work, providing an overview of:

➤ the activities pupils undertake in Support Groups
➤ the involvement of the wider staff within the school
➤ how parents are encouraged to support their children
➤ how Support Group Leaders are trained and supported

## The activities pupils undertake in Support Groups

Pupils engage in a variety of activities within Support Groups and this chapter serves to place them within context and offers some exemplification. Materials are provided on the CD Rom and a sample can be found in Chapter 7.

Activities fall within three categories:

■ individual, negotiated target-setting

■ collaborative tasks that foster group discussion

■ completion of the Support Group Diary.

### Individual, negotiated target-setting: the process

Target-setting is fundamental to the approach for a number of reasons, as set out at the top of p. 13. Target-setting can take two forms – short- or long-term – and, indeed, there is no reason why both approaches cannot be implemented simultaneously. Short-term targets are set weekly (though monitored daily) and long-term targets are set to cover a period of a month or term. The long-term target is designed by the Support Group Leader in negotiation with the pupil, specifically to meet the needs of the pupil (see example at bottom of p. 13). This takes the form of a card, which can be taken home, and/or a small, laminated, pocket-sized version, which can be carried around and used, discreetly, in classes.

## Target-setting

- ❑ It provides a mechanism through which pupils can be encouraged to take responsibility for their own behaviour.

- ❑ It encourages pupils to reflect upon their behaviour.

- ❑ It fosters intra-personal intelligence as pupils gradually develop insight into their behaviour.

- ❑ It provides the opportunity for the Support Group Leader to open discussion about behaviour in a positive way.

- ❑ It enables a 'step-by-step' approach to be adopted, commencing with smaller, more easily achievable targets leading to more encompassing targets such as, 'To take a more positive attitude towards my work'.

- ❑ It enables the pupil, parent and Support Group Leader to have an overview of progress.

- ❑ It fosters communication between the classroom teacher and pupil, parent and Support Group Leader.

- ❑ It provides a channel of communication for the pupil and parent.

- ❑ It fosters the transfer of what is learned within the group to the wider school environment in that it encourages pupils not only to reflect back upon their experiences but also to look forward to what needs to be accomplished in the future.

## An individually negotiated long-term target. The pupil's coloured card shows 'traffic lights' red, amber and green[1]

**PLEASE DO NOT TALK**

STOP, CALM DOWN AND THINK!

Am I able to concentrate upon my work?
Am I preventing others from working?
Am I annoying other people?
What else can I do?

DO THE RIGHT THING!

Both processes involve negotiation between the Support Group Leader and the pupil, requiring the co-operation of the pupil. It is therefore very important for the Support Group Leader, at the initial meeting of the group, to share with the group the purpose of the exercise and for pupils to take ownership of this process therefore the targets are set *by the pupil*, with the advice of the Support Group Leader.

In relation to short-term target-setting, targets are reviewed and set between the pupil and Support Group Leader at the beginning of each group session and ten minutes should be set aside for the group to settle and for targets to be set. These targets are then written onto the front page of the target-booklet (which has a page for each day of the week) or, if a daily card (see advice to follow), at the top of the card (see example on p. 15). A few minutes should also be set aside at the end of the session for the Support Group Leader to write a comment in the target-booklet on the progress of each pupil in reaching his/her own target during the group session.

Whilst this target-card has been devised for use in a Secondary school, working to a six-period day, it could easily be adapted to a different context, and a weekly card for Primary use (using the same format) can be found on the CD Rom. Advice for the completion of target-cards is printed on the back of the card or behind the front-cover of the weekly target-booklet.

There are several important features in the design of this card. Whilst it may appear similar to monitoring systems in place in other schools, it does not use a rating scheme. There are several reasons for this: rating schemes (whilst initially appearing a simple, straight-forward and quick option) present a range of difficulties. Firstly, and most importantly, whilst they may convey an overview of a pupil's behaviour over the course of a day, they give no explanation as to why a child may have been rated favourably or poorly. This is not helpful in an approach such as this, which is based upon helping pupils to understand the nature of the difficulties they face in the classroom and around the school, and nor is it informative for parents. Secondly, rating schemes are not a reliable means of recording a pupil's progress. Even when a rating scale is provided, one teacher's 'A' is another teacher's 'B' and there is no means of the pupil or parent distinguishing between them. For these reasons, it was decided to use a 'comments only' system.

Another important feature of the card is the option it provides for teachers to comment on aspects of the pupil's behaviour or work attitude other than the target set; thus, a pupil who may have fulfilled his/her target ('arriving in class on time') but who has otherwise not behaved well, is more likely to have that achievement acknowledged even if, in other respects, he/she has fallen short of expectation. Likewise, a pupil who has failed to meet his/her target but has, in other ways, performed well, can have these other, more positive, aspects drawn to attention. This option to comment fulfils another very important function – it helps the pupil and Support Group Leader to identify future targets.

Pupils are asked to hand their target-booklets to the class teacher(s) at the *beginning* of each lesson (this is important as the class teacher should be monitoring the progress of the pupil against the target set) and to collect them at the end of the lesson. It is important also to prepare pupils to deal with negative comments in a positive way as otherwise the target-setting in itself could provoke aggressive behaviour.

The booklets should be monitored daily by the Support Group Leader at a time and place that is suited to the individual concerned and, if necessary, pupils can be issued with slips giving them permission to leave class and asking them to report to their Support Group Leader. In

# Example of a Pupil Support Card

## Pupil Support Card

Issued by:                Date

TARGET

Tick if you consider that the pupil has met the target.

*Only comment if considered necessary

| Period | √ | Subject | Comment on Target | General Comment* | Sig. |
|--------|---|---------|-------------------|------------------|------|
| p1 | | | | | |
| p2 | | | | | |
| p3 | | | | | |
| p4 | | | | | |
| p5 | | | | | |
| p6 | | | | | |

Support Group Leader's  Comment

Pupil's  Comment

Parent's  Comment

practice, most Support Group Leaders monitor the progress of pupils during morning registration. Register/Form teachers may also be willing to take on this role, liaising with the Support Group Leader. It is advisable not to ask pupils to report at times that they would regard as 'their time' – intervals, lunch hours etc. – as this is likely to lead to a lack of co-operation.

There is provision for pupils to be able to write their own comments on their progress, although there is no onus upon them to do so. The booklets should then be taken home for parents to be able to scrutinise the pupil's progress over the day and for them to comment in the space provided, if they wish to do so. In the event of a child who is very disorganised, the Support Group Leader will gather in the daily cards over the course of the week and send them in the post to the parent at the end of the week.

For reasons elaborated upon in Chapter 4 (see Motivational theory) a 'carrot and stick' approach is not advocated within the target-setting process; there is no external reward promised to pupils if they achieve certain targets. However, a distinction can be made between a genuine demonstration of appreciation, as in letters sent, unprompted, by one Support Group Leader to parents of pupils who were making extraordinary progress (see below) and in the occasional use of 'gold stars'.

> *You'd have thought it was a gold medal from the Olympics – he was so chuffed and so was I. He gets excited about nothing but it's hanging on the wall in the kitchen.* (Thomas's mother)

## Individual, negotiated target-setting: the nature of targets set

What form should targets take? Targets should, ideally, be:

- Relevant to the needs of the pupil.

- Specific and expressed, where possible, in positive terms (thus, ' put your hand up to speak' is preferable to 'don't shout out'). The exception is targets where it is too convoluted to express the target positively or there is no direct parallel to the message to be conveyed.

- Achievable, thus, as already indicated, building up in small steps. Smaller targets may be embedded within larger ones (for example, 'don't talk in class' could be one of the steps on the way to 'allow others to learn').

- Should gradually shift in focus from behaviour to learning-related outcomes, for example, 'to concentrate in class'.

- Should, in some cases, reflect the needs of others within the classroom, as in the example given above.

Whilst there are parallels between these guidelines and those of S (specific), M (measurable), A (achievable), R (relevant), T (time-measured) targets, the emphasis is placed less upon outcomes as it is the participation within the target-setting process which is of the essence in developing self-responsibility in pupils.

Pupils do not always find it easy to identify targets, as their problems are often multi-faceted. It is tempting, but counter-productive, in these circumstances to set more general, all-embracing targets, such as 'behave in class', and, indeed, there is a need to educate the wider staff as to the nature and aims of the target-setting process as, in the experience of the author, there was a lack of understanding of the need for a staged and incremental approach. To facilitate this process, the author, in consultation with Support Group Leaders, produced a card from which pupils could select appropriate targets. As the example below shows, the targets are divided into four quadrants and the teacher, through a process of questioning, would help the pupil to identify a quadrant initially and then a target from the quadrant.

## Example of Support Group Targets

### Support Group Targets

| *Showing Consideration* | *Developing Learning Habits* |
|---|---|
| Put up my hand when I want to speak<br>Keep still in class – don't fidget<br>Keep quiet in class – don't talk<br>Co-operate with what the teacher is asking me to do<br>Organise myself at the beginning of the lesson – take off jacket etc.<br>Try to think of the needs of others to learn | Bring the correct equipment to class<br>Do homework as well as I can<br>Try to concentrate upon my work<br>Listen carefully to the teacher<br>Ask for help if I get stuck<br>Keep trying if I get stuck<br>Arrive for class on time<br>Do my best work |
| *Developing Good Relationships* | *Developing Self-Control and Self-Responsibility* |
| Listen to other people – don't interrupt<br>Be kind to other people<br>Avoid getting into arguments – walk away or visualise traffic lights<br>Be polite to teachers<br>Treat other people the way I want to be treated | Try to keep calm in class<br>Think before I act<br>Accept that I am at fault when I have done something wrong<br>Say sorry if I have done something wrong<br>Keep calm if I get into trouble<br>Behave responsibly around the school e.g. don't drop litter<br>Behave in a sensible, mature way |

## Reflections upon the target-setting process

Support Group Leaders supported the target-setting process in principle but, as might be expected, indicated that there were difficulties, at times, in getting pupils to co-operate by reporting for monitoring with a fully completed card. Some pupils tended to 'lose' the card if they had had an unfavourable report and others just lacked the organisational skills to be able to remember to collect the card at the end of each lesson or to return it from home. It was recommended that these pupils should be issued with daily monitoring cards. There were also a small number of pupils who did not respond positively to this form of monitoring.

*Really did not like this type of monitoring. He found the Support Group discussions sometimes too probing, too personal.* (SG Leader)

These issues were discussed at the regular meetings held with Support Group Leaders and a range of options were put into practice to try to alleviate these difficulties, which will be elaborated upon in Chapter 6. However, there were many instances of Support Group Leaders reporting upon the favourable responses of pupils to the target-setting process and the beneficial effect which this had had on pupil progress. It is clear from some of the comments made by pupils that target-setting had had a positive effect:

*In the booklet you were able to choose your own target and it was one that you wanted to work on. Made everything feel alright.*

*The teachers were able to write exactly what you had got into trouble for – more detailed than the conduct cards. In the group you'd all sit down and say what you'd done wrong and explain it to each other and say how you wouldn't do it again.*

**Case study: Stewart**

Stewart was described by his Support Group Leader as being 'extremely co-operative', displaying a maturity 'more sometimes than I would have imagined. I have all his weekly booklets signed by parents and teachers'. Stewart's family considered that the target-booklet had been an excellent support which had enabled them to see, on a daily basis, how Stewart was progressing. Stewart also reported that the target-setting had helped: 'It was clearly said what you had to do and teachers could easily check'. Over time, his reports from class teachers gradually improved.

(Derived from interviews with Stewart, his family, guidance teacher and SG Leader. Stewart is a pseudonym)

## Collaborative tasks that foster group discussion

Group work is organised around a series of tasks – some related directly to the classroom situation, some related to peer relationships and others that are open-ended in nature and can lead discussion in a range of different directions. The tasks are all designed to promote reflection and understanding in pupils of their values, beliefs and motivations and of their inter-personal relationships. They are not designed to inculcate a set of establishment values (although no activity in which people engage can be thought of as bias-free) but to enable pupils to form their own judgements based upon critical evaluation. They are designed also to promote thinking skills in that the capacity to exercise judgement and to think creatively (what other options do I have?) are central to the transferability of what has been learned within the Support Group to the classroom situation, the wider context of the school and the daily lives of pupils. In undertaking these tasks within the supportive environment of the group, pupils are also developing their inter-personal and communication skills under the guidance of the Support Group Leader.

Tasks can take a variety of forms:

- the use of scenarios to prompt discussion

- compare and contrast

- prioritisation exercises

- role-reversal

- ordering, sorting and classification exercises

- creative activities

- analytical and evaluative activities

- planning activities.

In addition, a series of Information Sheets introduces pupils to new concepts and ideas as a means of helping them to further their knowledge and understanding and provides a support to the activities. The activities are varied and require the active involvement of pupils and, whilst they may require some initial writing as pupils clarify their thinking, are mostly concerned with group discussion.

## Completion of the Support Group Diary

The diary (see example on p. 20) is a tool to help pupils to reflect upon and learn from their experiences, whether positive or negative. Pupils complete their diaries within the group, reflecting upon a situation they have experienced in the course of the week. The diary consists of a series of prompts that lead the pupil through the incident and a vocabulary is provided at the front from which they can draw. The diary is completed in writing and the Support Group Leader takes the opportunity, as others write, to talk through the incidents individually with each pupil. It is not the written record which is important but the process of discussion.

The role of the Support Group Leader is to support and challenge. To *support* the pupils through a process that might be quite distressing for them (much as they might not admit it) but also to *challenge* by probing beneath the surface of the pupil's entries (a process described by David Perkins (see Chapters 3, 4 and 6) as 'Socratic Questioning') to encourage them to think much more deeply about the issues: What makes you think that the teacher's picking on you? Is that really how you felt at the time? How else could you have reacted?

Some Support Group Leaders like to use the diary at the beginning of the session (after the target-setting process) but, if it is used in this way, it is important to impose a time limit (perhaps exploring in depth only the diary entry of one pupil on each occasion). As trust builds up in the group, pupils may be willing to share their diary entries with others within the group but this should always be at the discretion of the pupil. Other Support Group Leaders intersperse it with group activities, particularly if it is felt that there is a specific need for it – perhaps one of the pupils in the group has had a 'less than successful' week or someone has had a success that they wish to share with the others. It can be very useful when pupils are absent and the group has only one or two pupils within it, allowing for the more in-depth attention which the diary requires.

# Example of Support Group Diary: a series of prompts lead the pupil through the incident

## Support Group Diary

Describe the situation

- where were you and who were you with?
- when did it occur?
- how had you been feeling before the incident occurred?
- what happened?

How did other people react to you at the time?

- what did they do?
- how did they feel?

How did you react at the time?

- what did you do?
- how did you feel?

What were the consequences for you and others?

How did you feel after the event?

- did you understand why it had happened?

What have you learned from the experience?

- what would you do if you were faced with the same situation again?

---

### Support Group Diary

Describe the situation

How did other people react to you at the time?

How did you react at the time?

What were the consequences for you and others?

How did you feel after the event?

What have you learned from the experience?

### Reflections upon the use of the Support Group Diary

The extent to which Support Group Leaders used the diary varied considerably, with some finding it a very useful resource and others, whilst acknowledging its value, finding it quite a demanding exercise because of the need for one-to-one attention with each pupil. It is within this scenario that a senior pupil mentor or learning auxiliary, who sits in with and assists with the group, can be very useful.

One pupil provided a good exemplification of how use of the diary had helped him:

*The diary helped because, in discussions, it helped to deal with situations, [for example] how you [Support Group Leader] told us it takes a man to fight but a bigger man if you can walk away from the confrontation.*

---

**Reflection Point**

Do you feel that the approaches described could be of value to your pupils? What benefits would you hope they would be able to gain from participation? (You might want to think about specific pupils.)

---

## The involvement of the wider staff within the school

In practical terms, the involvement of the wider staff in the school might appear quite slight in that they are directly involved essentially in just two processes – target-setting (as previously described) and in the completion of a questionnaire at the end of the intervention asking them to comment upon the progress of each pupil who has been involved within it.

However, this would be to grossly under-estimate the essential role classroom teachers play in supporting pupils through the intervention. If teachers take the view that pupils are beyond redemption and that the only way to deal with misbehaviour is through sanctions then the likelihood of pupils' succeeding would be minimal. Fortunately, in my experience, with a few exceptions, most classroom teachers, if they perceive that a pupil is trying to improve, will be supportive of this process. This highlights the need for training of *all* staff within the school, including non-teaching staff with whom pupils will come into contact (learning auxiliaries, office staff, home-support workers ... ), about the aims and methodologies of the approach.

Such an approach was adopted within the school and a 2-hour session was set aside during an in-service training day in which all staff received a short presentation about the work of the Support Groups and were then sub-divided into small groups, led by Support Group Leaders, in which the approaches were exemplified, providing an opportunity for questions to be raised and for group discussion. This training was very well received and prompted a great deal of staff interest (and, indeed, a few additional staff volunteers).

## How parents are encouraged to support their children

Parents are encouraged to support their children in a variety of ways: through the target-setting process; through building upon and re-inforcing this process at home; and, most importantly, by taking an interest in their child's progress and encouraging them. The initial parents' meeting is one of the principal vehicles for conveying this message as is the 'Support Group Leaflet for Parents' (see CD Rom), which is sent in the post to each parent along with the letter seeking permission for pupil participation.

However, many of the parents of the pupils involved within the Support Groups have quite frequent contact with Pastoral Care/Guidance staff and senior management within the school, and the opportunity is taken to raise issues relating to the Support Group on these occasions.

## How Support Group Leaders are trained and supported

The training and induction process is extensive and consists of several elements:

- An initial 2–3-hour session (negotiated with senior management) in which Support Group Leaders are introduced to the theories underlying the approach, the Support Group Leaders' Guidelines, pupil materials and means of pupil assessment. This also provides the opportunity for Support Group Leaders to raise any questions or issues.

- Induction of new staff through the support of a more experienced Support Group Leader team-teaching through the first four weeks of the intervention, gradually passing over control to the new recruit. The importance of this cannot be under-estimated as Support Group work is quite different in nature from working with full-sized classes or even one-to-one counselling. By observing how the more experienced Support Group Leader interacts with the group and sets appropriate boundaries for the group, the new recruit can gradually gain in confidence.

- Ongoing support for all members of the team through the Project Leader regularly 'popping' into groups and taking an interest in the activities. This also conveys an important message to staff and pupils that their efforts are valued.

- Regular meetings specifically devoted to 'housekeeping' issues such as the monitoring of pupil attendance, management of the target-setting process etc.

- Meetings devoted specifically to the sharing of good practice and preparing Support Group Leaders for the activities to follow.

- Ongoing in-service training as considered necessary (for example, on the conduct of pupil interviews).

Meetings were generally negotiated between myself and the Support Group Leaders and took place either on in-service training days, during periods when there were fewer demands upon the timetable, for example when pupils were on examination leave or during lunch times (lunch being provided by the school). They generally took place fortnightly and were an important means of forging a 'team spirit'. Clearly, the training and support provided for Support Group Leaders is a very important issue and is a theme which is developed further in Chapter 8.

**Summary**

This chapter has provided a broad overview of the approaches adopted within Support Group work and drawn from the experience of staff, parents and pupils. A whole-school approach, consulting with and involving all staff in the school, is advocated, as is high-quality staff training. The forging of good partnership working with parents is also key to success.

## CHAPTER 3

# The Aims of the Approach

This chapter provides an overview of:

➤ why it is important to teach for understanding
➤ the characteristics of pupils within the study, prior to intervention
➤ the desired outcomes for pupils
➤ the research questions that guide the research evaluative study

In working with children with SEBD there are many possible approaches that can be of value, depending upon the desired aims and outcomes. The approach adopted will reflect the belief and value system held by the individual and the understanding and life experiences which that individual brings to the decision-making process. For example, if the problem is believed to lie with children's inability to control their emotions then an anger management approach, focusing upon the development of strategies to manage distressing moods, will be adopted. If, however, the problem is thought to lie with children's inability to express emotions then an emotional literacy approach, introducing children to the vocabulary and concept of emotions, will be adopted. Likewise, if the problem is perceived as resulting from a lack of self-esteem the focus will be upon positive thinking and strategies such as visualisation.

All of the above approaches have one thing in common – they are all deficit models, conceiving of the problem as lying within the child – the child 'needs fixing'. Some would argue that a deficit model is not appropriate, seeing the problem as a systems failure, reflected in:

■ inappropriate curricula

■ poor management/leadership

■ ineffective, badly thought-out policies (or lack of)

■ inadequacies in staff understanding and skills

■ ineffective pastoral care systems

■ poor school ethos.

Seen in these terms, a 'systems' approach is likely to be adopted, with solutions such as more flexible, responsive curricula and a focus upon leadership and policies, upon systems for the delivery of pastoral care, and upon staff training.

Others argue that the problem lies outwith the school situation, in the family or in the community. Relevant factors, amongst others, in that case would be:

- child poverty

- poor health

- family issues (domestic violence, child neglect, substance abuse ... )

- social immobility (lack of training or employment prospects; poor uptake of further or higher education)

all of which can lead potentially to diminished life chances. Solutions in this case are likely to be political, linking to the discourse on social capital,[1] social inclusion and the need for inter-agency/partnership working. The national 'respect' agenda arises from this understanding of the problem. Whilst there is a tendency for polarised positions to be adopted, it is likely that the problem rests within all of these areas, which implies that, if success is to be achieved, the solution rests in addressing all of them – it is a matter of balance.

The diagram on p. 26 illustrates the range of factors (relating to the child; school systems and policy; and influences external to the school (including Government policy)) which impact upon the problem and which therefore need to be taken account of in arriving at a solution.

Whilst academics may argue for one perspective over another, from a pragmatic point of view the question for a practising professional must be, 'How can I make a difference?' Whilst it may be the case that a focus upon policy and systemic factors is ultimately the best, long-term solution, change takes time and children have only one chance at their education. The bottom line has to be – to what extent have I been able to make a difference to the life and life chances of this child?

**Reflection Point**

Where do you stand on these issues? Where do you see the problem lying? Do you agree with the stance taken in the above paragraph? How do you feel that you can make a difference?

The approach adopted in Support Group work takes cognisance of the various approaches towards working with children with SEBD and draws upon them to an extent, and also emphasises the whole-school perspective, focusing upon policy, practice and school ethos, but its principal focus is upon the development of understanding in children of themselves, of others and of their inter-personal relationships.

## Why teach for understanding?

A child might be able to learn strategies for anger management and even have an understanding of the physiological processes that occur in the body when under stress. This does not necessarily

# Factors that impinge on SEBD

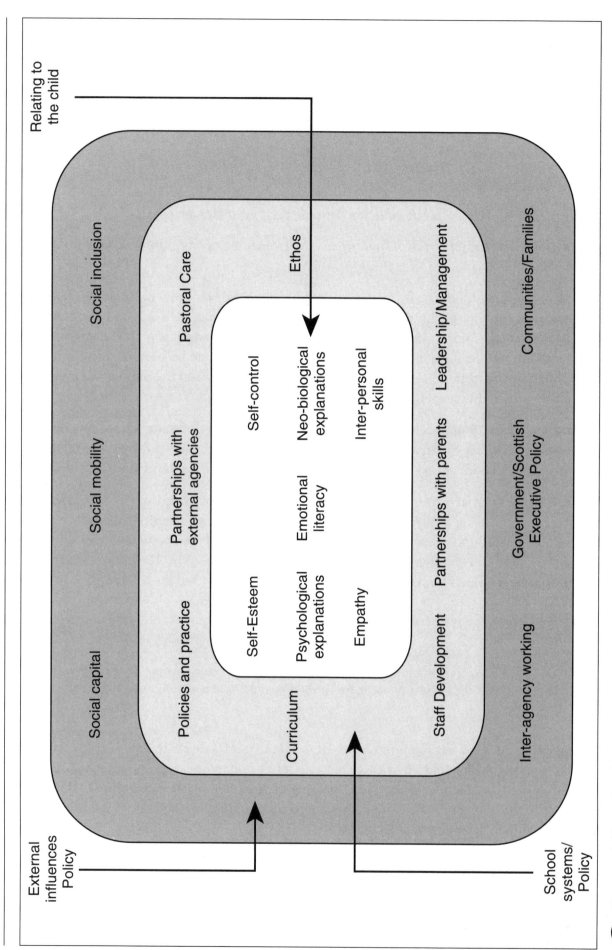

translate into effective action if the child has little understanding of his or her own emotions (and the beliefs and goals that drive emotions) or those of others – if the child does not understand the 'triggers' of his anger and the effects on others.

A child may develop inter-personal skills but if he lacks empathy (which arises from having an understanding of self and of others – a *theory of mind*)[2] they are of limited value. Likewise, a child may develop 'emotional intelligence' but, if she uses these capacities to seek advantage over others, it might better be called 'manipulative intelligence'. Some bullies are highly adept socially. Gardner (1999) makes a clear distinction between an intelligence and what one does with that intelligence – it can be put to good or bad use. Thus, morality is distinct from the concept of intelligence.

Does developing emotional literacy necessarily translate into compassion and empathy? Does thinking positively necessarily bring results if, in other respects, the child is not provided with the means to realise his or her goals?

These approaches do have their place and they have been of great value to many individuals but in themselves they are insufficient. If children are to effect change in their lives, they have to reach an understanding of the forces that operate upon them and upon others, and that ultimately guide their actions. Having gained insight, they are then in a position to benefit from the range of other approaches and to make meaningful choices in their lives.

## The central role of understanding

The search for meaning is central to our existence and is part of what it means to be human. From our earliest moments we seek to make sense of our world, to 'make connections' that enable us to develop cognitive skills – to think, to be creative and to reason; to grow physically, socially and emotionally. Yet, the development of understanding is not only a cognitive process but a product of the social and cultural experiences which shape our lives. Brewer, in her study of the development of children's thinking processes, states:

> Children's thinking does not take place in a vacuum – it is influenced by other people from day one. Equally, social progress cannot take place without the ability to think, reason and learn. (Brewer, 2001: 8)

Vygotsky (1978) characterises learning as being primarily a collaborative venture in which an adult mediates the learning process for the child (acting as the stepping stone between the learner and the learning source), scaffolding the learning (building it up incrementally). The Support Group Leader mediates children's learning by helping them to 'make connections' between new knowledge and what they already know and are familiar with, and between new knowledge and its applications for their daily lives. The Support Group Leader then scaffolds that learning through a process of staged collaborative tasks and through a process of Socratic Questioning (see Chapters 4 and 6).

If we bring these various threads together, they all point to the need for the quest for understanding to be conceived as an essential, central process that is cultivated within a social and cultural context.

What exactly do we mean by 'understanding'? This question is not as straight-forward as it first appears, as there are conflicting views as to what constitutes understanding. Our use of everyday language suggests that it is sometimes conceived as a passive representation – 'I see what you mean' – almost like a photograph. Claxton (1998) argues for understanding as partially intuitive – arising from unconscious perception (sensations that do not register at a conscious level) – that 'Eureka' moment! Psychologists forward the concepts of mental models (representations within our heads – a mental 'picture') and action schema (latent representations that guide our actions – an 'executive function') as being the means by which we make sense of the information processed by our brains, connecting the incoming information to what is already known and understood.

These are complex concepts, well beyond the boundaries of this book to explore. Perkins (1993) and Gardner (1993a), on the other hand, argue for understanding to be conceptualised as a performance – an *active mental process* – one in which understanding is both developed and demonstrated through doing. If a student were to write an essay on the causes of the First World War, he would be developing his understanding through having to engage with and analyse the ideas, synthesising and ordering those ideas to make a convincing, coherent argument. This is a description of process. However, in so doing, he would also be demonstrating his understanding to others through the product which he has created. Perkins and Gardner describe such manifestations of the development and demonstration of understanding as being *understanding performances.*

## Reflection Point

Which of these conceptions of understanding do you find most useful in helping you to develop an understanding of how your pupils learn and process new information to form their understanding? Do you share the view, which I expressed, that understanding is an essential element of living?

Within the literature pertaining to 'Teaching for Understanding' there are many definitions of understanding as being an active mental process, but perhaps the most pertinent to Support Group work is this definition:

> Teaching for understanding – the view that what students learn needs to be internalised, able to be used in many different circumstances in and out of classrooms, serving as a base for ongoing and extended learning, always alive with possibilities. (Perrone, 1997: 13)

## Reflection Point

Can you think of 'understanding performances' in relation to your teaching or your own learning? Can you think of ways in which you currently mediate the learning process for others and scaffold their learning?

## Developing a theory of mind

Having come to the realisation that the need is for children to develop an understanding of themselves and others, the question arises as to what makes up one's sense of identity? What are the various constituents of the individual which make him or her unique?

In my view, the constituent parts are:

- beliefs (what I hold to be true)

- values (what I hold to be right – the principles which guide my life)

- motivations (my goals and aspirations)

- attitudes (the opinions/prejudices which I hold, which derive from my emotions and value and belief systems), which underlie motivations.

It is important to note that these are personal to the individual – a belief, value, motivation or attitude may or may not be shared by others. This is a very powerful message to give to children as it is saying that actions are determined by these other variables and it therefore follows that if one were to change any or all of these variables it can impact upon our actions. It is saying to children, 'You can change'. It gives children a sense of agency in their lives which is not contingent upon rewards or sanctions.

However, gaining an understanding of oneself is only half of the story. Without a capacity to understand that one has a mind which is constituted of feelings, beliefs etc. and that others also have these capacities, which are different from our own, a child is locked into his or her own world, unable to understand the feelings, motivations or belief/value systems of others and therefore unable to develop the capacity for empathy which underlies effective inter-personal relationships. This capacity to discern the moods, temperaments, motivations and intentions of others is what Gardner describes as inter-personal intelligence (Gardner, 1993a: 240).

Some psychologists describe the capacity to understand the relationship between one's own and others' mental and emotional states as a 'theory of mind'. Gardner, when he returns to his original writing on the theory of multiple intelligence (1993), acknowledges the important role which having a theory of mind plays in a child's capacity for both inter-personal and intra-personal intelligence, the latter of which he describes as:

> ... the capacity to understand oneself, to have an effective working model of oneself – including one's own desires, fears, and capacities – and to use such information effectively in regulating one's own life. (Gardner, 1999: 43)

A 'working model of oneself' which serves as a guide for self-regulation is an important aspect of a theory of mind.

Brewer (2001) describes an experiment in which a child (who has witnessed his mother replace pennies from a piggy bank with marbles) is asked what another child (who did not witness this event) would be likely to reply when asked, 'What do you think is inside the piggy bank?' A child answering 'Pennies' would have developed a theory of mind.

## The aims of the approach as they relate to the evaluative study

The aims of the approach are reflected in the desired outcomes for pupils (to follow) and are also reflected within the aims and research questions of the evaluative study, the latter of which are outlined in the section to follow. The means by which the study was conducted and of establishing the statistical significance of the findings are described in the Chapter Notes (see p. 103).

# What are the desired outcomes for pupils?

Following on from the previous discussion, the first outcome is related to the development in the pupil of intra- and inter-personal intelligence as is described in research question 1:

*(1) Is teaching for understanding happening?*

To what extent have pupils succeeded or failed in developing an understanding of self (attitudes, beliefs, values and motivations), of others and of their inter-personal relationships?

If it can be established that 'teaching for understanding' is happening, the next question has to be 'Does it make a difference?' and, if so, in which respects?

Beyond developing the capacities for intra- and inter-personal intelligences, Support Group work aims to develop further in children their capacities for empathy and to form and maintain good inter-personal relationships. It was significant to note that, referring back to the reasons for which pupils were nominated to Support Groups, the principal responses related to poor inter-personal relationships – defiant, aggressive behaviour characterised by a lack of consideration for others. There were highly significant differences between Support Group pupils (prior to intervention) and a group of pupils within the same year group who were not involved in the initiative between how they rated themselves in respect of their inter-personal relationships, particularly in relation to how they perceived their own behaviour towards others.

One of the goals inherent in Gardner's theory of intra-personal intelligence is that individuals through gaining insight into their emotions will gain the capacity to self-regulate their behaviour. Other respects in which Support Group pupils rated themselves less favourably than the comparator group were in relation to their concepts of their own behaviour, their capacity to understand the motivations behind it and their ability to control it.

Two further areas in which significant differences emerged between the two groups were in relation to pupils' perceptions of themselves as being effective learners and their capacity to persevere when experiencing difficulty. As might be expected, the responses of Support Group pupils were less positive in both these respects.

There are clear resonances between the desired outcomes for Support Group pupils and Goleman's theory of emotional intelligence. Goleman (1996) identifies five emotional and social competencies – self-awareness, self-regulation, motivation, empathy and social skills. His concept of emotional intelligence will be explored further in Chapter 4.

*(2) Does it make a difference?*

To what extent (if any) have pupils been able to develop and demonstrate improvement in their:

❑ ability to regulate their behaviour with good judgement in a range of contexts?

❑ capacity for empathy and ability to relate well to others?

❑ confidence and self-esteem?

❑ development of habits of mind, beliefs, feelings and behaviour which dispose them towards effective learning and which impact upon their attitudes towards learning and school?

These are very ambitious goals, and one has to be realistic in terms of outcome in taking account of the life experiences pupils have accumulated and the many influences on their lives, including the media, not all of which are positive. However, some of our young people are at risk of becoming increasingly disenfranchised and alienated from society, which poses a real threat not only to themselves but to others in the community and to society at large. Support Group pupils:

■ had an average attendance rate in Year 8/S1 of 78% in comparison to their peers within the same year groups, whose attendance rate was 93%

■ accounted for more than half of all unauthorized absence in Year 8/S1 (inclusive of exclusions) of the year group yet represented only 9% of that year group

■ accounted for around half of all serious (recorded) incidents of indiscipline which had been referred to senior management; the differentials in Year 9/S2 (term 1) in relation to the total number of referrals and the frequency and duration of suspensions in comparison to their peers within the year group were statistically highly significant

■ were performing well below their expected level of attainment in National Tests in Year 7/Primary 7, 20% having reached only the level in reading, and 36% the level in writing, expected of most pupils in the course of Primary 4 to Primary 6.

Whilst some of the statistics relating to attendance and discipline are not entirely unexpected given the criteria by which pupils are selected for Support Groups, what is of particular note is the link with attainment. It should be borne in mind, however, that there are wide variations within the Support Group population in respect of each of these measures.

Social inclusion is a major issue that needs to be tackled on all fronts and at all levels. One of the most important goals of Support Group work therefore is to support children within the system and to give them a lifeline. These wider concerns were reflected in the final two research questions of the study, which focus on the variables that might affect the outcomes for individual pupils and upon the significance of the work in relation to national imperatives – such as *A Curriculum for Excellence* (SEED, 2004a) and the National Priorities (SEED, 2000a).

*(3)   The variables which affect pupil outcome*

What are the strengths and weaknesses of the approach?

❑   If, through participation in Support Groups, an effect has been observed, whether positive or negative, how is it accounted for by the individual pupil and others?

❑   Does the effect apply equally to all pupils? What factors might be forwarded to explain any variability in effect?

❑   Does it last over time? How does the pupil perceive the experience of participating within the Support Group in retrospect?

*(4)   What is its significance?*

In which ways does the Support Group Initiative address current priorities and imperatives within Scottish Education?

The Case Study which follows illustrates the impact of the SGI upon Thomas, a pupil experiencing severe difficulties prior to intervention, as described by a range of stakeholders – his parents, class teachers, Support Group Leader and Thomas himself.

## Case study: Thomas

Prior to intervention, Thomas was experiencing severe difficulties in coping with school life. In a four-month period he had been referred for serious indiscipline on 30 occasions and had been suspended from school on nine occasions for a total of 23 days. His mother no longer felt there was any point in attending further interviews with the school. Thomas was not nominated for the Support Group by his Guidance teacher, who considered Thomas was beyond being able to benefit from it. I persuaded him to nominate Thomas for a group.

Contrary to expectation, Thomas responded very positively – ... *realised that you could change things 'yerself'*. In contrast to his previous record, Thomas was suspended only once, for four days, after his involvement in the Support Group. Thomas's Guidance teacher was very pleased with his progress – *key is that someone took an interest in him. The group gave him time out from coursework to think about self. Don't think they ever get the chance to do this*. His Support Group Leader considered that Thomas had made a very positive contribution towards the group – *Never dominated group. Took other contributions on board. Helps draw out other pupils*. Class teachers were more mixed in their responses but there was no doubt that Thomas's mother was delighted with his progress – *He needs a prop. If there was no group, no yourself [author], he would have gone from bad to worse.*

(Derived from interviews with Thomas, his Guidance teacher, Support Group Leader and mother. Thomas is a pseudonym).

## Summary

In addressing the difficulties posed by children with SEBD, the solution lies in addressing the needs of the individual child for additional support and in systemic and political solutions. I put forward the case that 'teaching for understanding' lies at the heart of enabling pupils to make meaningful choices in their lives, leading to a sense of agency. Enabling pupils to develop further their intra- and inter-personal intelligences means they are better placed to lay the foundations for empathy and inter-personal skills and to develop the capacity to self-regulate their behaviour.

It is also hoped that, in the process, pupils will also develop in confidence and self-esteem and will develop further learning dispositions (such as the capacity to persevere when encountering difficulties), which will enable them to develop more positive attitudes towards learning and towards school. These aims are reflected in the questions posed by the evaluative study: Is teaching for understanding happening? If so, does it make a difference?

However, perhaps of even greater importance is the need to provide an inclusive environment in which pupils do not become disenfranchised from the system and alienated from society. The final two questions address these issues and seek to evaluate the efficacy of the approach, identifying the variables that affect outcome for individual pupils.

# THE CONTEXT OF SUPPORT GROUP WORK

## CHAPTER 4

# The Influences Underlying the Approach

This chapter provides an outline of the influences that underlie the approach:

➢ teaching for understanding
➢ thinking skills
➢ concepts of intelligence
➢ motivational theory

## Teaching for understanding

A group of scholars at Harvard Graduate School of Education, led by David Perkins, Howard Gardner and Vito Perrone, working within 'Project Zero', set up a collaborative project with schools in which they established a framework that could be used to promote deeper and more meaningful learning. Support Group activities are organised around this framework.

Whilst there have been previous attempts by scholars to create curricula for schools, what distinguishes this approach is that it does not provide a rigid curriculum but guidelines around which a curriculum can be framed. The *Teaching for Understanding Framework* identifies four principal elements, which are outlined on p. 36.

Perkins believes that the development of understanding is principally concerned with encouraging learners to work with their knowledge in thoughtful ways and it is through working with knowledge in a range of different activities that the learner not only gains understanding but is also able to demonstrate it, which he describes as *understanding performances*:

> Understanding is being able to carry out a variety of actions or 'performances' that show one's grasp of a topic and at the same time advance it. It is being able to take knowledge and use it in new ways. (Perkins, 1998: 13)

## The Teaching for Understanding Framework (derived from Perkins et al., 1998, in Wiske(ed))

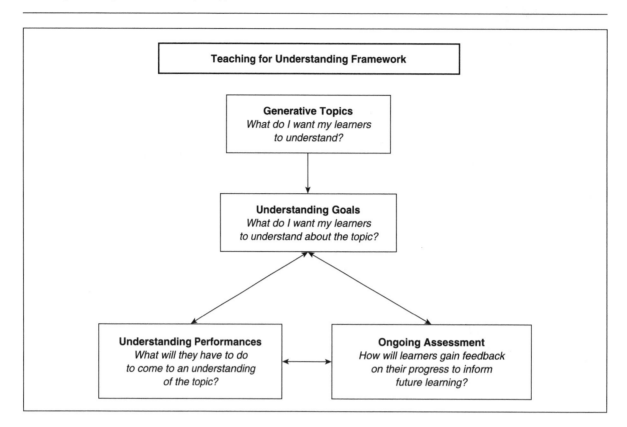

Perkins stresses the importance of *generative topics* – topics that are central to the subject discipline and are not only intrinsically motivating for learners but, as previously quoted, provide scope for meaningful engagement, which develops deeper understanding and insights. This conflicts with an approach in which 'coverage' is of the essence and in which coverage is equated with learning.

He stresses the important role of teachers in helping pupils to make connections between new and prior learning, to applications within other subject disciplines and within their daily lives to maximise the transferability and applications of learning. He describes this as a process of *bridging* and also identifies the process of *hugging* (keeping the instruction as close to the desired end-product as possible, for example, if the aim is to develop an understanding of the need to examine and balance evidence in History, this is best undertaken by enquiry in which pupils have the opportunity to apply these skills) (Perkins and Salomon, 2001).

Perkins sees the role of the teacher as being one in which he or she, through developing thinking skills and devising carefully thought-out tasks with clearly defined goals (*understanding goals*) and a process of *ongoing assessment* to encourage critical reflection on learning, leads the pupil to a new level of understanding – *'to press learners to think well beyond what they already know'* (Perkins and Blythe, 1994: 7). Perkins is arguing for a curriculum that is less content-based, more flexible and creates room for more thoughtful and meaningful engagement in learning.

Parallel to the application of the framework, Perkins strongly advocates the development of *thinking skills* and *metacognition* – the capacity of individuals to be able to reflect upon their own learning processes[1] – as he believes that it is only through the development of thinking skills that pupils gain the capacity to apply their new learning to different contexts with good judgement and it is only through the gaining of understanding and insight into the processes of learning that one is able to learn effectively.

## What is the significance of the Teaching for Understanding Framework for Support Group work?

Support Group work offers the ideal context in which to apply these principles. In a setting in which there is a very high teacher/pupil ratio there is scope in which to develop the thinking skills which Perkins advocates. In addition, the absence of an external syllabus provides the teacher leading the group with the opportunity to create and explore *generative topics* in which:

- Issues of relevance to the pupils and which provide scope for meaningful learning can be explored in depth.

- The responses pupils provide can be developed and probed in a supportive environment and pupils can be asked to explain and justify their opinions and otherwise develop their capacities for creative and critical thinking and problem-solving. By this means, the Support Group Leader *scaffolds* (see Chapter 3) their learning.

- The Support Group leader *mediates* the learning of pupils through the use of the Support Group Diary, helping them to reflect retrospectively (what happened?) and prospectively (what would you do differently the next time?) – a process Perkins and Salomon call *high transfer* (Perkins and Salomon, 2001). This process is more likely to result in pupils being able to apply their learning gained in one context (the Support Group) to another (the classroom/around the school/at home).

- Pupils are encouraged to make explicit connections between their learning and their life experiences within and outwith school.

- There is the flexibility to explore issues which might arise in discussion.

Many of the above are also exemplifications of *understanding performances.*

The process of *bridging* is facilitated by target-setting in which the Support Group Leader encourages the pupil to put into practice the principles that emerge within the groups and monitors the pupil's progress in relation to these targets on a daily basis. This process can also be facilitated by the Support Group Leader in the day-to-day dealings with the pupil, making connections between the discussions that take place within the group and classroom/around school discussion and, if raised by the pupil, home-based incidents.

As previously described, the fundamental aim of Support Group work is to develop in children understanding of themselves and others (Gardner's *personal intelligences*) and of their inter-personal relationships such that it can impact upon their behaviour, their self-esteem, learning dispositions and attitudes towards school (see Chapter 3). These are therefore the *understanding goals* that underlie the project. In addition, pupils are encouraged to reflect upon how they learn and the factors which, for them as individuals, hinder or promote effective learning, fostering *metacognition*. Pupils gain insight into their learning through *ongoing assessment* by:

- feedback obtained from class teachers through the target-setting process

- opportunities for critical reflection in discussion of their pupil diaries

- responses to the pupil's contributions to group discussion and tasks

- opportunities for experiential learning arising from collaborative problem-solving within the group

- formal feedback from their Support Group Leader drawing upon a wide range of evidence (see Chapter 8).

# Thinking skills

Thinking skills are generally categorised as being of three principal types – *critical thinking, creative thinking* and *problem-solving*. The dividing line between these three types is less clear-cut than one might imagine. For example, in the process of musical composition all three types of thinking are involved:

- *creative thinking* in the sense that the composer has to generate ideas that form the basis of the composition and develop them with imagination

- *critical thinking* in the sense that the composer has to evaluate these ideas and decide which of them are worthy of development

- *problem-solving* in that the process of composition is one of constantly having to make decisions that impact upon each other, often in complex ways.

Within each subject discipline, there will be examples of activities that draw upon each of these types of thinking. It is also argued that thinking skills are, to an extent, context-based. What might be regarded as problem-solving in Maths may be quite different from problem-solving in Science, although there may be parallels.

## Why are thinking skills important?

If, as Perkins maintains, we wish to 'press learners to think well beyond what they already know', it is imperative to foster *higher-order thinking skills,* such as evaluative and analytical skills. Likewise, with the emphasis upon lifelong learning and the need to produce adaptable and flexible young people, a focus upon creative and critical thinking skills and problem-solving is essential.

## What are the implications for Support Groups?

In relating the field of thinking skills to Support Group work, I drew upon the work of Carol McGuinness (the *Activating Children's Thinking Skills (ACTS) Programme*) (see p. 39), which, in turn, builds upon the work of Swartz and Parks (1994).

**The ACTS programme (with kind permission of Carol McGuiness, *Teaching and Learning Research Briefing* no. 18, ESRC)**

# ACTS (Activating Children's Thinking Skills)

*Searching for Meaning*

- ☐ sequencing, ordering, ranking
- ☐ sorting, grouping, classifying
- ☐ analysing, identifying parts and wholes
- ☐ noting similarities and differences
- ☐ finding patterns and relationships
- ☐ comparing and contrasting

*Problem-Solving*

- ☐ analysing and clarifying solutions
- ☐ generating alternative solutions
- ☐ selecting and implementing a solution strategy
- ☐ evaluating and checking how well a solution solves a problem

*Creative Thinking*

- ☐ generating ideas and possibilities
- ☐ building and combining ideas
- ☐ formulating own points of view
- ☐ taking multiple perspectives and seeing other points of view

*Critical Thinking*

- ☐ making predictions and formulating hypothesis
- ☐ drawing conclusions, giving reasons
- ☐ distinguishing fact from opinion
- ☐ determining bias, reliability of evidence
- ☐ relating cause and effects
- ☐ designing a fair test

*Metacognition*

- ☐ planning
- ☐ monitoring
- ☐ reflecting
- ☐ evaluating

*Decision-Making*

- ☐ identifying why a decision is necessary
- ☐ generating options
- ☐ predicting the likely consequences
- ☐ weighing up the pros and cons
- ☐ deciding on a course of action
- ☐ reviewing the consequences

One of the principal objectives of Support Groups is that they should foster understanding in pupils of their values, beliefs and attitudes; of how these values, beliefs and attitudes impact upon others; and of how they affect basic motivations and behaviour. This can only be achieved if pupils are encouraged to make those values, beliefs and attitudes explicit through engagement in discussion and thoughtful tasks. Hence, fostering thinking skills is crucial.

However, building upon an important point relating to the transferability of insights and skills so gained, it is crucial to help pupils to 'make the connection' by making explicit the applications of new insights by relating them to the immediate and prospective circumstances of the pupil, for example, classroom situations, interactions with others. The processes of *bridging*, *hugging* and *high transfer*, to which reference has already been made, help to achieve this aim. Embedding thinking skills within the Support Group approach is the most appropriate means of achieving this end.

# Concepts of intelligence

The past few decades have seen a major shift in how intelligence is conceptualised. The traditional view of intelligence as being largely innate, fixed and based upon a narrow range of competencies, principally concerned with language and problem-solving – what might be described as *general intelligence* ($g$) – is being challenged by the work of Howard Gardner, who is one of a number of psychologists who are developing new ways of thinking about intelligence. Gardner is not arguing that $g$ does not exist but that intelligence manifests itself in a range of forms and is perceived, valued and measured by different cultures in different ways. Thus, in some cultures, *spatial* intelligence would be of greater significance than *logical-mathematical* intelligence.

Whilst there is heated debate amongst psychologists about the varied claims made, these new developments have been very useful in raising the awareness of educators of the issues that impact upon how children learn and therefore impact upon how teachers should teach, and many teachers have embraced the ideas with enthusiasm.

## Multiple intelligence theory (MI theory)

Gardner proposes that intelligence is not fixed (and can therefore be developed) and that it is based upon a much wider range of competencies than has previously been understood to be the case. Of the eight (potentially nine) intelligences that Gardner puts forward, the two personal intelligences (which relate closely to the concept of theory of mind), *intra-* and *inter-personal* intelligence, are the most relevant for Support Group work, although it also draws upon *linguistic* and *logical-mathematical* intelligences.

The real significance of Gardner's theory lies in his recognition of individual difference and of human potential.

> We are not all the same; we do not all have the same kind of minds ... ; and education works most effectively if these differences are taken into account rather than denied or ignored. (Gardner, 1999: 91)

From my perspective, the essence of the theory is to respect the many differences among people, the multiple variations in the ways that they learn, the several modes by which they can be assessed, and the almost infinite number of ways in which they can leave a mark on the world. (Gardner, 2000: Preface)

Gardner is giving teachers a clear message. However, he is not advocating that teachers should seek to categorise their learners according to the different intelligences and nor is he suggesting that teachers should be trying to achieve the impossible through attempting to deliver each aspect of what they teach through each of the intelligences. Rather, he is advocating a flexible, imaginative approach that takes account of individual difference, drawing upon the range of intelligences as seems appropriate.

---

**Reflection Point**

The tendency to think of people as being either clever or not is part of our culture. Think of the many colloquial expressions to suggest that a person is not intelligent – 'not quite the full shilling' etc. To what extent, as a teacher, have you been influenced by this perspective? Do you tend to form impressions of your pupils as either being able or not able? Does this influence how you interact with them? Might it influence outcome?

---

## A focus on the personal intelligences

Gardner introduces his two personal intelligences together because he maintains that, whilst they can be regarded as distinct from each other, they are also inter-dependent: we gain an understanding of self through our interactions with others but those interactions are coloured by our understanding of self and of others. Rather like a chicken and an egg! He suggests that one's sense of personal identity comes from a fusion of the two personal intelligences – they mutually modify each other. However, Gardner also draws attention to the important role played by culture and the development of language in the child's developing self concept.

it is through the learning – and use – of the symbol system of one's culture that personal intelligences come to assume their characteristic form. (Gardner, 1993: 275)

The capacity to develop a theory of mind is an essential component in the development of empathy. It is only by this means that a child can perceive the world from a range of perspectives and understand the intentions of others. Brewer sums this up very effectively in her statement,

We live in a world full of individuals who think, feel and act according to their view of what is happening around them. In order to survive in this complex social environment, and to interact with other people in an acceptable way, we have to learn to understand the world from other people's perspectives. It is only by standing in their shoes like this that we can hope to understand the intentions behind their actions, and judge how to respond appropriately. (Brewer, 2001: 15)

These are essential skills for all people, but, in particular, for children with SEBD. Might it be the case that some children whose behaviour is often perceived by others as self-centred, selfish and inconsiderate may not have a theory of mind consistent with their stage of development – lacking the capacity to reflect upon their behaviour; failing to understand the potential impact of their behaviour on others and therefore lacking a capacity to understand the consequences of their behaviour for themselves and others?

**Reflection Point**

Would you agree with this hypothesis advanced above? Whilst I am not arguing that, in every case, an undeveloped theory of mind may underlie the difficulties experienced by the young person, might it be a useful way of thinking about our work with young people? How does this accord with your own understanding and experience? Can you think of children for whom this might be the case?

## What is the significance of MI theory for Support Group work?

Chapter 3 explored the aims of Support Group work and it is evident that the child's capacity to develop further the personal intelligences and capacity for empathy is key to the approach. Many of the activities promote the child's ability to perceive a range of perspectives and Support Group Leaders will actively encourage this process by sharing with pupils the difficulties they face as teachers and the emotions they feel.

## Emotional intelligence theory

Goleman describes *emotional intelligence* as constituting:

> abilities such as being able to motivate oneself and persist in the face of frustrations; to control impulse and to delay gratification; to regulate one's moods and keep distress from swamping the ability to think; to empathise and to hope. (Goleman, 1996: 34)

Whilst Goleman's work can be criticised on the basis that it is questionable as to whether his conception is an 'intelligence' (the same arguments are often directed towards Gardner's work) and on the basis that he builds much of his argument on anecdotal evidence, I believe that his work is of value in that it recognises the role emotions can play in cognitive function. It is also important to recognise that all emotions – whether positive or negative – play an important function in alerting us to potentially difficult or dangerous situations (nagging doubts are often well-founded even if we can't quite 'put our finger' on their cause) and to potentially beneficial situations, and therefore play an important function in helping to guide our actions (if, sometimes, in a subtle way). Goleman's work clearly resonates very closely with the desired aims for Support Group pupils.

## Motivational theory

Amongst the aims identified in Chapter 3 were the further development in pupils of self-esteem, learning dispositions and more positive attitudes towards learning and school. The concepts of self-esteem, self-efficacy (a sense of being able to do something) and motivation are closely inter-related and all have a bearing upon those aims.

Whilst much attention has been directed towards the development of self-esteem (which Lawrence (2002) describes as the difference between how we perceive ourselves, as reflected in the mirror of others' perceptions of us, and how we would like to be), the work of Dweck and Elliot (1983) and McLean (2003) would indicate that the concept of self-efficacy is of at least equal importance in explaining pupils' motivation towards learning.

Motivation is generally categorised as extrinsic (influenced by factors external to the individual) or intrinsic (arising from factors within the individual). There is a body of evidence to indicate that extrinsic motivation, whilst it may bring about short-term gains, is harmful in the long term as it is contingent upon tokens of esteem, leading to unstable self-esteem in the recipient. (Imagine a situation in which the 'tokens' awarded are dependent upon the mood of the parent or teacher or are suddenly withdrawn.) Khon (1999) draws from research studies to indicate that people who have been extrinsically rewarded show less inclination to continue with the activity after the reward has been withdrawn than those who have had no reward. McLean (2003) identifies that pupils with contingent self-esteem may be over-dependent upon feedback from others and may react adversely to constructive criticism. Having an internal sense of self-efficacy is of greater value to these pupils.

However, this leaves the question as to how to foster self-efficacy and intrinsic motivation? Dweck and Elliot (1983), drawing from previous theories of motivation, put forward a new theory which rests on the premise that motivation towards learning may rest initially in the conceptions people hold about their intelligence – are they entity learners? (people who believe that intelligence is innate and fixed – you've either 'got it' or you ain't!) or are they incremental learners? (a belief that through effort and by incremental stages, people can build upon their capacities and intelligence). It is clear that people who hold an incremental perspective are more likely to be motivated in the face of the difficulties that all learners experience and are more likely to persevere and to problem-solve (examples of learning dispositions). Those who hold an *entity* perspective and who lack a sense of self-efficacy, Dweck (2002) describes as having *maladaptive* (*helpless*) patterns of achievement, and those with an *incremental* perspective, *adaptive* (*mastery orientated*) patterns.

---

**Reflection Point**

It became evident in working with Support Group pupils over the years that many of them held *maladaptive* (*helpless*) patterns of achievement. How would you characterise the patterns of some of the pupils with whom you work whom you would consider to be disaffected? Do they believe that, with effort and the application of appropriate learning strategies, they can succeed in their learning or will further effort confirm their views of themselves as being unable to learn, as identified by Entwistle (1987)?

What changes would be needed to policy and practice within your school to break the *maladaptive* pattern? What changes can you make within your classroom to foster *mastery orientated* patterns of achievement?

---

McLean (2003) advocates:

> Teachers can, for example, encourage students to think of ability as changeable and encourage them to adopt a mastery attitude and to make optimistic explanations for their success that help build their confidence. (McLean, 2003: 51)

He is not advocating that teachers should praise pupils for work well below their capabilities in an effort to promote 'positive thinking', which, in my experience, is a strategy most pupils see through.

## What are the implications for Support Group work?

The implications are clear. Support Group Leaders need to work with pupils and their families to promote reflection in pupils about how they learn (*metacognition*) and to encourage them to develop a view of themselves in which they can see that, with appropriate effort and the use of appropriate learning strategies, they can build upon their learning. Pupils need to experience success in appropriate, attainable and yet challenging goals if a sense of self-efficacy is to develop, and the target-setting process is one of the mechanisms Support Group Leaders can use  in this respect. One of the activities is designed specifically to address these issues (Activity 2c, see CD Rom). This is an area, however, that needs to be addressed across the school for all learners, as Support Group Leaders working in isolation are likely to have limited impact.

### Summary

This chapter has explored the key ideas that influenced the development of Support Group work, drawing from theories of constructivist learning and teaching ('Teaching for Understanding'), teaching for transfer, thinking skills, theories of intelligence (and in particular the personal intelligences as described by Gardner) and theories of motivation, related to the concepts of self-esteem and self-efficacy. The chapter also explored the relevance of these theories to Support Group work, making the connection between theory and practice.

# Identifying and Meeting a Need

This chapter places Support Groups within the wider context of:

➤ the Children's Rights Movement
➤ social exclusion and its 'alter-ego', social inclusion
➤ special educational needs (SEN)/additional support needs (ASN) with specific reference to children with social and emotional behavioural difficulties (SEBD)
➤ a focus upon school discipline and ethos
➤ national and school-based interventions to foster inclusion, tackle indiscipline and to support children with SEBD.

*It's not just 'me, me, me' but them. Never used to think about it before. I used to think, 'Never mind everybody else – it's only me.'* (Support Group pupil)

The latter part of the twentieth century witnessed concerns about a perceived breakdown in society, producing a 'me, me, me' generation and changes in societal norms, such as the emergence of the 'ladette' culture expressed in the 40% rise of Scottish girls caught up in crime (*Glasgow Herald*, 2006); an increased focus upon anti-social behaviour (met with governmental responses such as the introduction of ASBOs (Anti-Social Behaviour Orders)) and an increasing clamour about indiscipline in schools, mirrored in lurid headlines and over-sensationalised portrayals of classroom life.

This has been paralleled with a growing concern for Children's Rights and a focus upon promoting social inclusion through removing the barriers that prevent people from being able to play a full role in society, with education perceived as being one of the principal means of achieving this end – hence the mantra, 'Education, education, education'. *Every Child Matters: Change for Children in Schools* (DfES, 2004a) sets out the government's agenda in this respect, paralleled with a plethora of initiatives UK-wide and reflected within the National Priorities (SEED, 2000a) and *A Curriculum for Excellence* (SEED, 2004a) in Scotland.

**Reflection Point**

Do you agree with these observations? Are there any other examples of changes in social norms which you have observed and which you feel may impact upon schools?

Given that the Support Group initiative developed within Scotland (in which education is a devolved function of the Scottish Parliament and therefore is distinct from that of the rest of the UK), this chapter explores both the perspective of the UK government (whilst recognising that each nation within the UK has a degree of autonomy in respect of policy and practice) and the Scottish Executive.

## A concern for children's rights

The concern for children's rights in the UK is part of a much wider concern for human rights in general and is part of a global movement. Children's rights are embedded within the *United Nations Convention of the Rights of the Child* (1989), which has been incorporated within the UK legislative framework. The 'Salamanca Statement' (UNESCO, 1994) is a global response to this quest, proclaiming a commitment to 'Education for All' (UNESCO, 1994, p. viii). The Salamanca Statement attests to the 'fundamental right to education' and the need for education systems to meet the wide diversity of characteristics and needs of children, including those with SEN.

## Social inclusion: why should we be concerned?

> Tackling Social Exclusion is at the heart of the government's mission. It is our fundamental belief that everyone should have the opportunity to achieve their potential in life. (Tony Blair, in 'Social Exclusion Task Force', 2006)

*Reaching Out: An Action Plan on Social Exclusion*, produced by the UK Government's Social Exclusion Task Force (2006), identifies that three million children in the UK are considered to be 'vulnerable' (that is, disadvantaged children who would benefit from extra help from public agencies). This represents more than 25% of all children within the UK. Of these, 26,000 in 2005 (based on DfES data) were on the Child Protection Register. The report indicates that children lacking in social and emotional skills are more likely in later life to be unemployed and/or involved in criminal activity. The report notes that when children lack these skills, they often disengage from schooling and the benefits that can be accrued from it.

In particular, there are concerns about socially disadvantaged groups (those who are likely to form the 'NEET' group – 'Not in Education, Employment or Training'). *Count us in: Achieving Inclusion in Scottish schools* (HMIE, 2002a) noted the 'significant numbers of young people who leave compulsory education without the intellectual and social skills which are necessary for adult life'. *Missing Out* (HMIE, 2006a) noted that amongst the 20% of lowest performing Scottish pupils the following groups were represented disproportionally – pupils entitled to free school meals, children in care, pupils with undeclared ethnicity, children with Record of Needs (RoN) (Statements) and boys.

# Towards more inclusive schooling: challenges and dilemmas

One of the findings to emerge consistently from studies of teachers' attitudes towards inclusion is that, whilst teachers support inclusion in principle, they have reservations about it in practice. In particular, there are concerns about the ability of schools to provide for the needs of children with complex emotional and behavioural needs. From having studied a wide range of literature in relation to this field, it is clear that there is no common understanding of what inclusion means. Interpretations range from the esoteric:

> about a sense, in our hearts perhaps, of being part of something such as an ideal; a belief system; humanity; the wider life world (Allan, 2004: 19)

to the equation of inclusion with a policy of placing children with SEN (UK Government)/ASN (Scottish Executive) within mainstream schools, as established within the survey conducted by the GTCS:

> Teachers mainly perceive the policy as being mainly about including every child in the mainstream school, irrespective of behaviour and irrespective of their effects on other pupils. (GTCS, 2005: 48)

This is paralleled with concerns about the role of Special Schools, as highlighted in some high profile cases within the media. It is clearly a very emotive issue which reaches to the heart of our fundamental beliefs and values. The difficulty with a concept such as inclusion is that it has an aura – a 'feel-good' factor – with which it is hard to disagree, rather like 'America and apple pie'. Baroness Warnock, in her recent return to the fray, argues for the need to critically evaluate policy and practice in relation to inclusion on the basis that she believes it does not meet the needs of some children.

In order to understand fully the argument that Baroness Warnock is making requires a historical perspective. The Warnock Report (DES, 1978) set in motion not only changes in policy and practice but a 'sea-change' in the ways in which disabled children were perceived within schools. The legislation arising from the report swept away categories of 'disabled' and 'normal' to be replaced with the single category of special educational needs (SEN) and introduced the process of statementing (RoN in Scotland) for those children considered to be in need of the greatest support.

Looking back on the implementation of the policy, the conception of the child as having 'needs' rather than disabilities (the medical model) led, in Warnock's view, to a failure to discriminate adequately between 'the differences not only between the educationally "needy" and others, but also between various kinds of educational need' (Warnock, 2005: 13). She goes on to state:

> If children's needs are to be met it is absolutely necessary to have ways of identifying not only what is needed but also why (by virtue of what condition or disability) it is needed. (Warnock, 2005: 21)

**Reflection Point**

Do you agree with the concerns raised by Mary Warnock? What would your definition of inclusion be?

Subsequent to the Warnock Report, there have been major shifts in thinking represented in the findings of the House of Commons cross-party working group examining the issue (House of Commons Education and Skills Committee, 2006), and changes in legislation in Scotland with the addition of the presumption of mainstreaming as an addendum to the Standards in Scotland's Schools etc. Act 2000 (SEED, 2000b) and the introduction of the Additional Support for Learning Act (SEED, 2004b), which introduced the concept of additional support needs (ASN).

The premise upon which the 'ASL' Act is based is that there is a need to move away from a 'deficit model' locating 'needs' within the child to a model in which there is a focus upon the additional support required in order for a child to thrive – a focus upon systems and practice. It is a 'social' rather than a 'medical' model. Additional support needs are conceptualised broadly to encompass the full range of support a child might require, whether temporary or permanent, for example in coping with the effects of bereavement. As such, it is conceptualised as pertaining potentially to all children at different stages of their school careers rather than to a narrow group of children, thus, in theory, reducing the stigma attached to the concept.

However, I would argue that what is required is a focus upon the difficulties likely to be experienced by the child, arising from the specific condition (enabling one to anticipate the barriers to learning the child is likely to encounter and to identify the support the child would require in order to overcome such barriers), in addition to a focus upon systems and practice and wider societal factors. It need not be one or other.

Warnock describes the experience of some children placed within mainstream schools as a 'painful kind of exclusion' which should not be imposed because of a political ideology. Lawson and her colleagues (2005) provide a poignant account of inclusion experienced as exclusion, as in this description of a child who has been removed from the classroom for disruptive behaviour:

> And you know, its pathetic, his little eyes looking in, it's almost like the whole of his life he's got this glass screen and he's looking in through the screen. (Lawson et al., 2005: 10)

I am not making the case that all children with SEN/ASN should be educated in Special Schools, nor am I suggesting that the policy of inclusion has not been successful in enhancing the life chances of many children. Indeed, many teachers testify to the positive effects of inclusion not only upon the children directly affected by the policy but upon all children within the setting. I am arguing that the concepts of exclusion and inclusion are much more complex than are often portrayed and that what matters is the child, on a case by case basis. It is not the location of schooling that matters but the sense of being included, of feeling valued and, most of all, being able to learn in an environment that is best suited to the needs of the child. This position is in keeping with the cross-party report on SEN (House of Commons Education and Skills Committee, 2006) which, in a highly critical critique of current policy and practice, attests to the 'mixed messages' emanating from government and argues for the needs of the individual child to be at the centre and for progress towards 'a system based on a range of high quality, well resourced, flexible provision to meet the needs of all children' (2006: 6). This is in keeping with the advocacy of a continuum of provision outlined in Audit Scotland/HMIE's 2003 report to the Scottish Executive.

The OFSTED report *Inclusion: Does It Matter Where Pupils Are Taught?* (DfES, 2006a) found that effective provision for children with learning difficulties and disabilities was distributed equally between mainstream and special schools when conditions such as the involvement of a specialist teacher, good assessment, work tailored to meet the needs of pupils and commitment and leadership from school management pertained.

**Reflection Point**

What are your views on these complex matters? Would you agree that an equation of *inclusion = mainstream school* and *exclusion = special school* (or some other form of extraction) is too simplistic and may not serve the needs of some children? What are your experiences of inclusion within your own school? Can you identify children who, whilst 'included' are not included at all, as described by Mary Warnock and in the study conducted by Lawson and her colleagues?

# A focus upon children with SEBD

Of particular concern in relation to this particular book was the finding within the OFSTED report that children with SEBD/BESD (behavioural, emotional and social difficulties) were particularly poorly served (DfEs, 2006a). The report identified that this specific group of children were less likely to receive support in the first place or to receive it too late. These findings are replicated in Scotland where it had been identified that children with SEBD were under-represented within the Special School population (prior to the implementation of the policy of 'presumption of mainstreaming') and were less likely in the first instance to have a RoN (Audit Scotland/HMIE, 2003). In a review of the policy of mainstreaming, Pirrie et al. (2006) report:

> The number of children traumatised by repeated failure in under-equipped mainstream settings is very high. Many would be able to integrate successfully if intervention was early and adequate. (Pirrie et al., 2006: 2.1.1)

Whilst Pirrie's comment is not specific to children with SEBD, many teachers will identify with this difficulty. However, the problem is even more fundamental than is indicated by the above. Many teachers feel that inclusion, particularly as it pertains to pupils with SEBD, is an agenda imposed from above with little account taken of the impact upon the classroom teacher and other pupils. The gap between those advocating inclusion on one hand and those on the 'delivery end' (and, in particular, class teachers) on the other is becoming wider, with voices in both camps becoming increasingly vociferous. This is obviously of great concern as the government's policies on social inclusion will only become a reality if they gain the 'hearts and minds' of the teaching profession. There is a need to engage with the profession, to listen to their concerns, to draw from their experience and to provide opportunities for teachers and their leaders to reflect upon and share their practice. The teacher voice not only needs to be listened to but given credence.

There is also a need to engage with and listen to the experiences of young people and their families, even those who would be critical of current practice, particularly in areas of social deprivation where the difficulties are likely to be intensified, as is indicated in the identification by John MacBeath (2006) of 'critical mass' as being an important concept in understanding the ability of schools to cope with the demands placed upon them in dealing with the difficulties posed by significant numbers of pupils with special needs (MacBeath et al., 2006, 7.1.28).

This failure to provide teachers with a sense of ownership has, in the view of some commentators, led to a culture in which some teachers disown themselves from the difficulties posed by children with SEBD, leading to a failure to acknowledge that pupils with SEBD are deserving of additional support, should be regarded as having SEN/ASN or have a right to have their opinions heard, as reported in many research studies. Hamill et al. (2002) report that:

> Many staff believe that the right to be treated in a caring way is forfeited by some young people as a consequence of their behaviour (2002: 42)

and accordingly believe that these young people have also lost their right to be treated with respect. Pirrie et al. draw from the views of a headteacher:

> One of the big problems in the mainstream classes … is persuading the teachers that these children should be there. (Pirrie et al., 2006: 4.2.1)

Studies of children who have been excluded from school often portray their experience of some teachers in a negative light (although many such pupils will identify individual teachers who have played a very positive role in trying to support them). They perceive some teachers as failing to treat pupils with respect, being unfair and rude, victimising and humiliating individual pupils, reflected in the concerns of pupils and their parents over the negative effects of labelling and being stigmatised because of their families or the locale in which they live. Riley et al. (2002), quoting from a female education worker, state:

> The main point that will stay with me is the fact that many of the young people recognise that their behaviour needs to change but cannot envisage the process of being able to change. Their behaviour is based on how staff expect them to behave. (2002: 40)

This statement illustrates the importance of intervention as a means of giving youngsters a vision and pathway, but it also illustrates the reciprocal relationship between low expectations and poor behaviour. Breaking free of this pattern is essential if pupils are to succeed. The role of the Support Group Leader in helping pupils to achieve this vision, to show them a pathway and to help them to break this negative cycle, cannot be under-estimated, but the roles of class teachers and senior management are crucial too.

Kendall et al. (2001), drawing from a range of studies by Kinder and colleagues (see, e.g., Kinder et al., 1996) characterise these negative observations of teacher behaviour (and observations such as, 'school's boring') by disaffected pupils as being part of a larger systemic breakdown between mainstream education and its pupils – a 'fight or flight' response by pupils to a discomfiting environment with which they cannot cope. These perceptions of some teachers by disaffected young people are replicated in many studies.

---

**Reflection Point**

To what extent does this account chime with your own experience? Whilst accepting that some children are not respectful in their relationships with other people, would you agree with the concerns of some pupils and their parents about the negative effects of labelling and stigmatization? If so, how might these difficulties be overcome?

Many studies have found that within the school setting the relationship between the young people and their teachers appeared to be of the essence. A report by SEED drawn from the voices of hard-to-reach groups (excluded pupils, their families and agencies working with them) (SEED, 2004c) identifies the most important aspect of support for a young person as being the establishment of a trustful relationship with 'an accessible, friendly and caring adult' (SEED, 2004c, 8.6). Likewise, the establishment of relationships characterised by mutual respect is also highlighted in various studies as being an important factor in preventing disaffection and/or effecting improvement in young people. Thus, there is a major job to be done in establishing a more positive and supportive ethos within mainstream schools if inclusion is to be ultimately successful.

## School discipline: should we be concerned?

> Most teachers are effective and committed to their task. Most schools deliver high quality learning opportunities to most pupils. … But 'most' is increasingly perceived by the profession and policy makers to be not enough. (GTCS, 2005: 7.7)

Concerns about school discipline are not new but they have come into sharper focus because of concerns about standards of conduct in society in general. It is generally agreed that the problems faced within schools are partially a reflection upon changes in societal norms and reflect problems within communities such as those associated with poverty, deprivation and substance abuse.

The raising of the school leaving age to 16 and the banning of corporal punishment in state-sector schools led to a focus upon school discipline resulting in the commissioning of a series of reports such as the 'Pack Report' (SED, 1977) and a series of research studies undertaken by the National Foundation of Educational Research (NFER) and Moray House (later to become part of Edinburgh University).

Consistent messages emerge from these research studies. In Scotland, the three surveys undertaken by Pamela Munn and her team (commissioned by the Scottish Executive and the teacher unions) paint a depressing picture of a 'drip, drip, drip' of persistent low-level disruption (as described by the authors), which eats at teacher morale and militates against effective learning. This is attributed by classroom teachers to a disruptive minority of pupils. Of even greater concern is the finding in the most recent survey (Munn et al., 2004) that, whilst much good work had been done within schools to promote good discipline and to create a positive ethos, there had been an increase in the number of Secondary teachers in particular reporting a wide range of potentially disruptive behaviours in and out of class, indicating problems with regard to pupil–pupil relationships but also pupil–teacher relationships. Three areas were highlighted by the authors:

■ the prevalence of boys in relation to concerns about indiscipline

■ the continuing effects of low-level disruption

■ the statistically significant rise in reports of physical aggression towards teachers (whilst still small, the trend is moving in the wrong direction).

The survey undertaken by Anne Wilkin and her colleagues (2006) on behalf of the Scottish Executive validates many of the findings of the Moray House/Edinburgh University surveys. However, a worrying development was the identification of an increase in the numbers of 3- to 4-year-olds entering mainstream education with complex difficulties and/or a lack of basic social skills. This is clearly of major concern, requiring an increased focus upon early intervention.

A study by Gillean McCluskey (2005) cautions that a much higher proportion of the 'generality' of pupils was involved in indiscipline than is indicated by national statistics on exclusion (particularly girls) and that the perceived distinction between the 'disruptive' and the 'disrupted' is not valid (whilst accepting that there may still be a 'troublesome minority'), thus questioning, in her view, restricted understandings of the problem which may lead to over-simplistic solutions.

The concerns about indiscipline are also backed up in the NUT-commissioned study *The Costs of Inclusion* (MacBeath et al., 2006), which is critical about inclusion as it is currently practised in England and Wales, and expresses concerns about the ability of schools to provide for pupils with complex emotional and behavioural needs, pointing out that the environment of the Secondary school in particular 'militates against the kind of emotional support and climate for learning that some young people need', leading to the imposition of inappropriate sanctions when they fail to cope with the strictures of the system (MacBeath et al., 2006: 7.1.4). This report indicates that statemented children were nine times more likely than their classmates to be permanently excluded from school, which can only be perceived as an indictment upon society. The GTCS survey also highlights similar concerns of classroom teachers who believe that a policy of inclusion (equated to a policy of 'mainstreaming') is not compatible with good school discipline nor with the 'standards agenda', highlighting, in particular, the need for smaller class sizes.

**Reflection Point**

Do you agree with the findings of the various surveys and studies to which reference has been made within this chapter in relation to school discipline? How does it accord with your experiences in the classroom and around the school?

I believe that teachers, pupils and parents are right to be concerned about school discipline but not in the over-sensationalised ways portrayed in the media. As indicated in the above quote, most schools go about their business effectively, often in very difficult circumstances, and most teachers and school leaders should be commended for their efforts and achievements in this regard.

## National and school-based strategies to tackle indiscipline and support children with SEBD

Whilst there are differences in emphasis and in approach between the UK Governmental and Scottish Executive responses to the dilemmas posed by indiscipline, there are also commonalities. UK Government and Scottish Executive initiatives are set out on p. 53. A very positive development has been the piloting and roll-out of initiatives such as 'Restorative Justice'; 'Framework for Intervention'/'Staged Intervention' (derived from the work initially undertaken in Birmingham); 'The Motivated School'; and the 'Solution Orientated School Programme' – an approach to promoting positive behaviour focusing upon the 'problem' and not the child. Other influential developments have been the establishment (within Scotland) of (formerly) the 'Ethos Network' and the 'Anti-Bullying Network' (operating from Edinburgh University) and the development of Circle Time approaches (Jenny Mosley) and Nurture Groups, primarily within Primary schools. Charitable bodies have also played a key role in developing initiatives, such as the pack of materials to promote inclusive practice in Primary schools developed by Barnardo's.

## Initiatives to promote positive discipline

| Promoting Positive Discipline | |
|---|---|
| *UK Government* | *Scottish Executive* |
| ❑ the commissioning of research e.g. Kinder et al., 1996 and 2000 | ❑ the commissioning of research e.g. Munn et al., 2000 and 2004. |
| ❑ the establishment of a Government Task Force leading to a National Charter setting out the rights and responsibilities of parents, pupils and teachers | ❑ the establishment of a Discipline Task Group leading to the publication of *Better Behaviour – Better Learning* (SEED, 2001b) |
| ❑ the embedding of behaviour and attendance within the National Strategy as exemplified within the Behaviour and Attendance strand for Key Stage 3 (DfES website) | ❑ the establishment of a 'Framework for Improvement' setting out National Priorities amongst which are 'Inclusion and Equality' and 'Framework for Learning' |
| ❑ the development of Early Intervention approaches, e.g. *Sure Start* | ❑ the development of Early Intervention approaches, e.g. *Sure Start* |
| ❑ the development of curricular programmes to be implemented nationally to address social and emotional learning, e.g. *SEAL* (DfES, 2005a) | ❑ the commissioning of a range of approaches to promote social and emotional learning, such as the 'Motivated School' |
| ❑ the promotion of a range of initiatives to promote Social Inclusion and school discipline as described in *Every Child Matters* (DfES, 2004a) and *Opportunity for All* (DWP, 2004) | ❑ the trialling of a range of approaches to promote positive discipline within schools, as described in *Connect* (SEED, 2004) |
| ❑ the establishment of children's trust arrangements to promote inter-agency working and integrated children's services (The Children Act, 2004, DfES, 2004b) | ❑ the establishment of Integrated Community Schools and advocacy of inter-agency working (*Happy, Safe and Achieving Their Potential*, SEED, 2005) |

The role Support Groups can play in addressing the issues that have been discussed within this chapter is described in Chapter 9. This chapter concludes, as it began, with the pupil voice:

*We got to the grass roots of why I was behaving the way I was. It taught me respect for people around me. Making a clown of myself – people laughing at me – not with me. Others are trying to learn – they don't need me disrupting them. (Support Group pupil)*

## Summary

This chapter has focused upon a wide range of issues, as described within the introduction. The devastating effects of social exclusion upon the life chances of young people are set out within this chapter, including the relationship between educational attainment, poverty, ethnicity, gender, unemployment and criminality. The chapter draws from a range of sources to make the case that the concepts of inclusion and exclusion are much more complex than often portrayed – that inclusion should not be equated with place but with a sense of belonging, of being valued and of being in an environment that promotes effective learning for the individual child. The chapter describes the changes in thinking that have led to developments within the field of SEN/ASL, outlining the different approaches adopted by the UK Government and the Scottish Executive. In particular, the concerns regarding the education of children with SEBD are explored and the case is made for much greater communication amongst and between all parties and for the need to develop a greater sense of ownership amongst school staff. Of key importance are respectful relationships, a positive school ethos and the creation of a climate that promotes effective learning.

The Government and the Scottish Executive (working in tandem with local authorities and charitable bodies) have been active in promoting positive discipline through the establishment of Task Forces leading to legislation (England)/the publication of *Better Behaviour – Better Learning* (Scotland); commissioned research; and the promotion of a range of initiatives, such as 'Restorative Justice'. Support groups clearly have an important role to play in promoting social inclusion and in taking forward the Government's recommendations in respect of pastoral care and school discipline.

# *I*MPLEMENTING THE APPROACH

## CHAPTER 6

# The Role of the Support Group Leader

This chapter explores the role of the Support Group Leader as facilitator, leader and manager of the group within the context of:

➢ establishing good relationships and a working ethos within groups
➢ keeping pupils on task, promoting deeper thinking and reflection whilst engaged in collaborative tasks

## Establishing good relationships and a working ethos within Support Groups

Central to the success of Support Group work is the quality of stewardship and leadership of the Support Group Leader. He or she is responsible for creating a climate of mutual respect through which pupils can flourish and develop the capacities desired of them. Whilst class teachers may have experience of group work within the context of whole-class teaching and Pastoral Care teachers may have experience of counselling children on a one-to-one basis, the dynamic of small-scale group work requires of the teacher a different set of skills, or a different emphasis in the use of those skills, which will be explored within this chapter.

If the Support Group Leader is to be ultimately successful in achieving the desired goals, he or she needs to mould a group of disparate individuals who may lack the social and communication skills to be able to function effectively as a team. Good teamwork is dependent upon having shared goals and purpose; the capacities to listen, to respect the views of others and to communicate in a respectful manner; upon consultation, collaboration and a willingness to give of oneself for the benefit of others. These attributes cannot be achieved through dictat. One of the important roles of the Support Group Leader is to:

■ model these capacities in his or her communications and practices within the group (the process of *hugging* (Perkins and Salomon, 2001) (see Chapter 4))

■ establish through consensus the working practices of the group via the Support Group Pledge (see p. 58 and CD Rom)

■ make clear the expectations he or she holds in relation to the contribution each pupil makes to the group and to hold pupils to account if they fail to meet these expectations.

## Example of the Support Group Pledge

---

*We promise to:*

*Treat anything said in the group as confidential*

*Show respect for each other*

*Don't mention teachers by name or talk disrespectfully about them*

*Keep all hands, feet, elbows, pencils etc. to yourself*

*Try to stay calm and avoid name calling*

*Listen to others and try not to interrupt*

*Work as a team*

---

The most important aspect of the Support Group Pledge is that it should be arrived at through consensus, involving all members of the group. The Support Group Leader should introduce the concept of the pledge by stressing the importance of good team work and co-operation – the concept that through working together on a common purpose much more can be achieved than through individual effort alone. The principal questions are:

■ How would you like your group to be?

■ How should we behave towards each other so that we can work effectively together?

The advice given should be that, where possible, the pledge should be expressed in desired behaviours rather than in a series of prohibitions, although convoluted statements should be avoided. Two possible approaches are:

■ the group could initially brainstorm ideas before evaluating and refining them

■ the group could be given an example of a Support Group Pledge as a starting point for discussion: Do you agree with these? Are there any you would miss out? Are there any missing? Which ones would you change?

There are two parts of the pledge which should not be negotiable, the first being the statement 'Don't mention teachers by name or talk disrespectfully about them'. There are important reasons for this, amongst them being that pupils should not be given the impression that being in the group gives them *carte blanche* to say anything they like about their teachers. It is only too easy in a group session for things to get out of hand and the simplest way to avoid this difficulty is to be up-front about it. It is important to gain the support of fellow members of staff in the school and if they consider that their reputations are being abused in this way, they would be unlikely to be supportive. This is not to imply that the concerns pupils have should not be taken seriously – they should be raised in an appropriate manner. Pupils generally understand the importance of this part of the pledge and, although there may be infringements, they are often not intentional. All that is required is a light-hearted reminder.

The second relates to confidentiality but it should be noted that, whilst in normal circumstances what is said in the group should be confidential, *in matters where child safety is an issue, the Support Group Leader has a duty to pass such information on to the appropriate channels within the school and pupils must be informed of this proviso.*

One of the most important aspects of the pledge is that it acts thereafter as a blueprint for expected behaviour within the group. It will require to be constantly re-inforced. Although a firm approach is required, it need not be heavy-handed. Experienced teachers know the value of humour in diffusing situations. A reminder as to why a statement was included in the pledge helps to re-inforce it not only for the pupil concerned but for the whole group.

Achieving shared goals and a common purpose is only possible if the Support Group Leader, in addition to leading the pupils through the programme incrementally, also gives pupils the 'bigger picture' – sharing with them the destination of their journey (the desired aims); the route they are going to take (explaining the programme to them); the role they are going to play in that journey (not passengers but active participants); and the role they can play in supporting each other. This needs to be re-inforced at all stages of the programme.

It is to be expected that the path to achieving these outcomes will not be a smooth one. Even the best of groups will experience a 'bumpy ride' and it is better to be prepared for this. MacGilchrist says:

> Real change – real improvement – is more likely to be associated with some pain and some conflict, especially if it is challenging a person's fundamental beliefs and attitudes. (MacGilchrist et al., 1997: 8)

The management of change will be discussed in greater depth in Chapter 8, but it is of value to draw upon Tuckman's theory of *forming* (the initial coming together of the team) (see in Everard and Morris, 1996: Fig. 10.3), *storming* (conflicting views and personalities emerge which need to be reconciled for the team to move forward); *norming* (the ways of working of the team becoming established); *re-forming* (a stage characterised by tension as people's positions and alliances change); and *performing* (the team working collaboratively and cohesively together). This model of how teams operate is of value in that it highlights that it is not necessarily a smooth process (even for highly skilled and committed adults). Perhaps it is because of the volatile nature of the individuals within Support Groups that the re-forming stage leading to performing is often re-visited and the journey can be perceived as a twisty, tortuous path leading to some dead-ends on the way. It can sometimes take only one pupil who has had an upsetting experience at home or in the previous class to upset the dynamic of the whole group. The Support Group Leader needs to be prepared for this and be ready to be flexible in approach, perhaps deviating from the planned lesson. (The Support Group Diary can prove to be a very useful resource in this circumstance.)

---

### Reflection Point

What is your experience of leading or participating in groups? Do you recognise the stages identified by Tuckman? What sorts of difficulties are likely to arise in trying to get the Support Group to work cohesively together with a common purpose? How might you anticipate and work pro-actively to try to avoid some of these difficulties?

---

The Support Group Leader needs to draw a fine line between a relaxed and inviting atmosphere in which purposeful activity takes place and one in which it is perceived that 'anything goes'. It was my observation that Support Group Leaders achieved this in different ways, reflecting their own personalities and belief and value systems. It is advisable to work within the norms that prevail within your establishment. If it is perceived that pupils attending groups are permitted to behave in ways that are not acceptable in other classes, there may be a backlash from staff who perceive (wrongly) that the Support Group is a 'soft option' or a reward for troublemakers. The right atmosphere can be created through:

- the warmth of the relationships between the Support Group Leader and pupils, reflecting care for the welfare of the individual pupil

  *We seem to get on – have a laugh. He comes to talk to me about things.* (SG Leader)

  *Made you feel welcome and it was amazing. He wasn't strict. Dead calm – you had a laugh and got to know him.* (SG pupil)

- the establishment of trust

  *It worked because I was able to trust the people in the group. If it had been a one-to-one, I would have felt awkward.* (SG pupil)

- the Support Group Leader being purposeful and well prepared for each session

- the inducement of pupils to support each other.

Whilst it cannot be expected that all pupils will respond in such a positive way, it is an indication that, given the right conditions being in place, improvement can be effected. As has previously been indicated, some pupils take longer than others to respond and these pupils can be difficult to manage in the earlier stages. It is to be expected that some pupils will not want to face up to the difficulties that they have and will find the discussions in the group intrusive.

*I hate people bringing up what I've done – I don't like being confronted with it.* (SG pupil)

In order to try to avoid these difficulties it is very important to brief pupils before involving them in the Support Group and to try to seek their co-operation, just as it is important to consult fully with their parents (as has been described in Chapter 1). If difficulties do present themselves, it is imperative that they should be tackled at an early stage. Firm handling of pupils within the groups and any necessary follow-up should be undertaken. The following are possible courses of action:

- Speak privately to the pupil prior to the next meeting of the group and try to ascertain whether there is an underlying cause for the poor behaviour. Take any necessary action arising from the discussion, liaising with other staff or parents, if required.

- Make it clear that high standards of behaviour are expected in the group and that action will be taken if there is no improvement.

- If there is no subsequent improvement, complete the *Area of Concern Form* (see p. 62 and CD Rom), which should be passed on to the Project Leader. The Area of Concern Form should trigger a further interview with the child and a communication with the parent, indicating that the pupil is not settling into the group as well as might have been expected. The Project Leader should then communicate with relevant personnel within the school.

- Involve other agencies such as Home–School Link workers, auxiliaries who normally work with the child.

- If there is still no improvement in the pupil's behaviour, a further Area of Concern Form should be completed and, at that stage, the parents should be invited to an interview and the pupil should be warned that further failure to comply could mean that he or she would be excluded from the group.

- If it is considered appropriate, bring into play the full range of mechanisms available to the school (after seeking the permission of the parents) (for example, the *Joint Assessment Team*, as previously described) such that the full range of professional perspectives can be focused upon the difficulty.

- As a final resort, offer the child the opportunity to withdraw from the Support Group (conditional upon a letter from the parent).

It is important to recognise that, even given the client group, it should rarely be necessary to carry out the full range of steps as described above. The majority of pupils, when they realise that action will be taken if they do not co-operate, begin to settle down.

# Area of Concern Form

Area of Concern Form

Pupil:                                         SGL:

Please describe below the nature of the concern:

Please tick below any previous action:

- ❑ initial interview with pupil
- ❑ further interview with pupil
- ❑ initial letter to parent
- ❑ further letter to parent (requesting interview)
- ❑ involvement of Pastoral Care/Senior Management
- ❑ involvement of other agencies (please detail below)
- ❑ other (please detail below)

*Any further comments*

*Signature of SGL:*                              *Date:*

Please pass to:

## Keeping pupils on task, promoting deeper thinking and reflection whilst engaged in collaborative tasks

One of the important respects in which Support Group work may differ from other programmes of work is that the tasks act as a vehicle to promote discussion and reflection rather than being solely ends in themselves, therefore a flexible approach needs to be adopted. It is not a matter of 'coverage'. There is no sense in which a Support Group Leader should feel under any obligation to deliver an activity within the time constraint of a lesson. It is desirable that activities should span as many lessons as it takes for the Support Group Leader to feel that the activity has fulfilled its purpose in enabling pupils to engage with the issues, keeping a careful eye on the responses of the pupils within the group. With experience, Support Group Leaders will learn to judge when it is time to move on to a different activity. For this reason, the tasks are described as activities and not lessons.

The Support Group Leader has to achieve a balance between 'going with the flow', letting the discussion develop, perhaps along a different path than the initial context, and a 'free for all' when the discussion drifts in an aimless way. As experienced teachers will attest, pupils can be very adept at this, especially if they wish to avoid the task. (It was interesting, however, to note that, in one session, it was one of the pupils in the group who brought everyone back to task.) At all times, the Support Group Leader (SGL) has to be tuned into looking for learning opportunities arising from the discussion, helping pupils to make connections to previous learning and to their daily lives, as in this excerpt from a transcript of a group in action:[1]

SGL:   *So you're saying that if you find the work that you're doing not very interesting, you might welcome a distraction? ...*

*How does that tie in with the card that we looked at a moment ago when we were all convinced that we wanted to learn? ... Can these two things come together?*

This type of questioning is an exemplification of the *higher-order thinking skills* advocated by Perkins and Blythe (1994: 7) in 'press[ing] learners to think well beyond what they already know' (a reference to Bruner). In asking pupils to respond to these questions, one is asking them to analyse, evaluate and justify their opinions and to weigh up and balance what would appear to be two contradictory statements as a means of formulating their own points of view (examples of both *critical* and *creative* thinking) (see Chapter 4). The Support Group Leader is acting to *scaffold* the thinking of the pupil, to help the child to conceptualise his or her learning and to build the vocabulary which enables the child to make sense of and communicate their experiences. However, this role is not solely that of the Support Group Leader. The Support Group, when pupils are actively engaged in activities and discussion, forms what might be described as a *learning community* in which members of that community learn from each other.[2]

Nuthall (2002) maintains that through participation in a learning community and the role of discourse within that community ('the activities, ways of thinking and relating to others that go with the talk within a specific community' – Nuthall, 2002: 53), individuals gradually take on the ways of thinking and being of the group. He therefore conceives of the role of the teacher as being to engage with the 'existing knowledge, beliefs and skills of the students' and through setting 'challenging problems and posing significant questions' to foster their learning (Nuthall, 2002: 47–48). Nuthall suggests that one of the means of achieving this outcome is through the teacher acting to scaffold the learning, model the learning process and create a climate for learning in which high expectations of student performance are crucial. A further means is the process of *reformulation* in which the teacher can build upon the contribution of the pupil, help to clarify the response and help the pupils participating within the discussion to discern the underlying threads of the discourse and its relevance to their learning. Thus, the Support Group Leader can take the contribution or response of the pupil, *reformulate* it and pass it back to the pupil, perhaps asking the pupil to clarify or justify the response further, to consider it from a different perspective or posing a question that encourages the pupil to engage with the concept at a deeper level.

M:    *I sometimes fool around and the class gets kept behind for it. I think they shouldn't.*

SGL:    *So you think that the whole class is getting punished for your behaviour and you think that's not fair? How do you feel when that happens, M?*

M:    *Angry.*

SGL:    *Angry with whom?*

M:    *The teacher for keeping the class behind for something I done.*

SGL:    *Do you feel any sense of responsibility in that situation? Do you feel any anger towards yourself or is it just the teacher?*

However, it cannot be assumed that as a result of discussion within the group that learning will automatically occur. The Support Group Leader supports the learning process through making the learning more explicit, perhaps by exploring in greater depth the concepts under discussion or summarising the learning of the group, as in this exemplification:

SGL:    *You've suggested that you lost a bit of self-respect. What else did you lose?*

M:    *My faith.*

SGL:    *Faith in what?*

M:    *My faith in myself.*

SGL:    *That's very good, M, that you were able to use that word. It's not quite the same as confidence. It's that a lack of faith in yourself leads to a lack of confidence. You've been doing very well recently in terms of your target and that's made you feel more confident and when you let yourself down you lose faith in yourself which makes you less confident.*

A further role the group fulfils is to enable misconceptions to surface. For example, within the 'respect' agenda, promoted by the Blair government, an assumption is made that all people share the same conception of respect. It has become evident in group discussion that this is not the case, as can be seen in this excerpt when a pupil describes how he answers back to his teacher when reprimanded:

D:    *The teacher respects you 'cos you're not going to let the teacher bully you.*

SGL:    *You're saying that the teacher respects you for answering back?*

D:    *So maybe the teacher that shouts at you wants to see how weak you are. [After further discussion]*

SGL:    *Do you think that it's true that teachers respect you more for saying, 'I didn't do that'?*

It can be seen from the above excerpt that pupils have been honest in their reflections upon what is difficult territory for them. This can be observed in their body language and sometimes in the brevity of the responses they give (often communicating with nods, rueful expressions, shrugged shoulders). It can be difficult, particularly with more reticent members of the group, to get pupils involved in discussion, and it is very tempting to rush in to fill in the gaps in the silence. However, it is imperative that this does not happen. Pupils need 'thinking time'. They need time to formulate their responses and to think through the issues. There are several ways in which the Support Group Leader can handle this situation:

- by offering to come back to the pupil once he has had time to think

- by simply pausing

- by reformulating the question and pausing again.

Another difficulty (which pertains to almost all group situations) is trying to ensure that the more vocal members of the group don't dominate to the detriment of others within the group. If this becomes a problem it could be addressed through the Support Group Pledge and, if necessary, by adapting it.

The group dynamic will vary depending upon the norms established in the group and some groups will be more relaxed than others, resulting in friendly (or not so friendly) banter. This need not be problematic if the Support Group Leader is skilled at handling it and can keep pupils on task. However, when it begins to interfere with the smooth running of the group, it can be very difficult. With younger groups, techniques such as those associated with 'Circle Time' (Mosley, 1998), in which pupils hold an object when making a contribution and then pass it on to the next contributor, can help the discussion to be more controlled and focused, but it is not a natural way for people to communicate and pupils should gradually be weaned off this way of communicating. Enthusiastic discussion will involve pupils occasionally talking over each other and interrupting each other, and as long as this remains within normal limits it should not be regarded as a problem. The child who either lacks the self-control to monitor his or her own contributions or who deliberately sets out to disrupt the contribution of others in the group (perhaps by shouting out inappropriate remarks) is a different 'kettle of fish' and needs to be handled firmly.

As has been referred to in previous chapters, a very important function of the Support Group Leader is to help pupils to understand the perspectives of others. This can be achieved by a variety of means:

- By trying to help pupils to understand the complexity of the role of the classroom teacher in managing the class effectively and creating a climate for learning through describing that role in the course of group discussion. This can help pupils to understand the basis of decisions which they sometimes consider to be unfair.

- By sharing with pupils your own ways of dealing with difficulties that present themselves within the classroom situation and how this makes you feel. (This may make you feel a little exposed but it is modelling what we are expecting of pupils within the groups and pupils will respect you for it.)

- By exploring explicitly with pupils the effect their actions are likely to have on others in real or potential situations

> SGL: *It would certainly have been very difficult for that teacher to deal with wouldn't it? You're [the teacher] just standing there waiting to teach a class and someone barges into your classroom.*

The role of the Support Group Leader can sometimes best be described as 'a dog with a bone', 'digging' away until the truth of the matter reveals itself. Contrast the beginning of the discussion relating to the incident that occurred in reference to the previous quote (a serious classroom fight):

SGL: *What do you think you lost from the situation, B?*
B: *[Long pause]*
SGL: *Did you lose anything?*
B: *mm … dunno … cannae think like …*

to the following:

SGL: *So one of the losses was that you disturbed other children's learning?   And it would have been very upsetting for the teacher to deal with. It was really a very aggressive situation then wasn't it?*
B: *Aye*
SGL: *So you really lost control of yourself, didn't you?*
B: *Aye.*

Whilst the answers of the pupil are monosyllabic, he is taking responsibility for his behaviour, beyond the 'mm … dunno … cannae think like' of his initial response

It could be very damaging emotionally, however, to lead pupils to an understanding of their difficulties without giving them a lifeline to help them to learn that there are other ways in which they can handle aggression and the other difficulties they face. Activities and Information Sheets are designed such as to develop pupils' understanding of these issues (for example, see Activity 3b and Information Sheet 9 in the Pupil Activities folder on the CD Rom).

A final and important point, Support Group Leaders, in the course of normal group work, will have to handle potentially sensitive and difficult issues. For example, in the course of legitimate group discussion, it may emerge that some of the practice of fellow colleagues, as described by pupils within the group, may not accord with your own ideas of good practice. It should never be assumed that pupils are exaggerating or lying, although, on occasion, this may prove to be the case. It is dishonest to imply to pupils that teachers will not occasionally get things wrong and, if you adopt the stance that 'teacher is always right' you are unlikely to get the co-operation of your group. It is important also to remember that you are not there in judgement of your colleagues and the best way you can handle this situation is to try to help pupils to understand the complexities of the situation and of their best means of handling it, as in the scenario below when a pupil is describing his reaction to a teacher telling him to 'shut up'.

SGL: *Was there anything wrong in the way you spoke to her?*
D: *… aye, I knew I was going to get into trouble for saying, 'Don't tell me to shut up'.*

SGL: ... *Why did you do that? Why did you go and do that?*

D: ... *Ah'm no gonna let her walk all over me.*

SGL: *You don't have to let her walk all over you. It shouldn't be a question of them and us.*

D: *Why do they get to ... ?*

SGL: *I'm not saying that what she said or did was right, but what I'm saying is that you need to look to yourself and say, 'What is the best way out of this?'*

Whilst the Support Group Leader is sympathetic to the situation in which the pupil has found himself and does not condone the actions of the teacher, she brings him back to the elements of the situation over which he can exert control. One of the activities pupils undertake is based upon Stephen Covey's concept of the 'Circle of Influence' (Covey, 2004) based upon the premise that effective people are those who work within the areas in which they can exert control (see Information Sheet 5 within the Pupil Activities folder in the CD Rom).

---

### Reflection Point

If you were faced with a similar scenario to that outlined in the last transcript, how might you have reacted? If you would handle it differently, explain why. (Keep in mind that Support Group Leaders have to 'think on their feet', as did the group leader in this scenario. Thinking through possible responses may help you to deal more effectively with future incidents.)

---

In the case of serious infringements that have been confided in you, *seek the advice immediately of a senior member of staff* and do not become involved at a personal level.

---

### Summary

The role of the Support Group Leader is crucial in establishing the ethos of the groups and an effective climate for learning. Central to these goals is the fostering of effective teamwork. The Support Group Pledge acts as a means of formulating the working practices of the group and is devised in consultation with pupils. Whilst every attempt should be made to 'bring pupils on board', trouble-shooting procedures have been identified to support the Support Group Leader. It is important for the group leader to share with pupils 'the big picture', as it is by this means that pupils can conceptualise their learning and be able to derive benefit from it.

The Support Group Leader uses a range of means to promote thinking and reflection, such as the use of probes and prompts and through reformulating pupil responses such that they can be explored in greater depth and built upon. Through participation in a Learning Community (Nuthall, 2002), pupils gradually assimilate the ways of thinking and being in the group. Another important facet of the group is to help pupils to understand the perspective of others and this is achieved in a variety of ways.

# Support Group Materials and Guidance for Their Implementation

This chapter provides:

➢ the 'housekeeping' arrangements for Support Groups

➢ an overview of the materials

➢ an introduction to the Support Group Leaders' Guide to Activities

➢ a sample of materials for Support Groups

➢ advice regarding assessment of pupil outcomes and materials to support the process

It should be noted that the full range of materials relating to all of the areas above can be accessed on the CD Rom.

## Housekeeping arrangements

### Organisation of materials

Individual files should be maintained by each Support Group Leader for each pupil within his or her group. A checklist of contents (see CD Rom) should be stapled onto the front of each folder. This enables the Support Group Leader to have an overview and record of pupil progress. Pupils should also be issued with individual folders in which they can keep their work, pupil diary and target-booklets which should be kept by the Support Group Leader.

The Project Leader should take responsibility for the duplication and organisation of pupil materials, which should be distributed to Support Group Leaders within box files. Instructions for duplication (as they pertain to each activity) are provided within the 'Support Group Leaders' Guide to Activities' (see CD Rom). Likewise, a folder in which the 'Guide to Activities' is interspersed with the pupil materials should be collated for Support Group Leaders (see index of Materials on CD Rom).

# Attendance

It is very important that pupils understand that regular attendance at the Support Group is important and that action will be taken if they fail to attend without good reason. However, be sensitive to issues. For example, on one occasion it was found that reluctance to attend was related to the pupils' missing their favourite class. In this case, the sensible action to take is to change the timing of the group. The following procedures should be observed:

■ a record of pupil attendance at the group should be kept

■ if the pupil fails to appear for the group, check initially with the attendance procedures at the school, and, if the pupil is marked present, contact the teacher of the class with whom the pupil would normally have been, requesting the attendance of the pupil at the group

■ if the pupil is marked present but cannot be found, alert the appropriate members of staff

■ if a pattern emerges of non-attendance, an *Area of Concern Form* should be completed (see Chapter 6 and CD Rom) and a staged set of procedures should be invoked.

Within the school, a decision was made, in consultation with senior management, that pupils on suspension from school should be allowed to attend the Support Group on condition that they were escorted onto and off the premises by a responsible adult. A letter to this effect was lodged with the school office staff who were asked to post it out along with the official letter of suspension. This decision was made on the basis that intermittent attendance at the Support Group would be likely to impede pupil progress. Whether this approach is adopted or not is open to the individual school but as it is a sensitive issue, it is important that proper consultation is carried out with all concerned parties.

# Monitoring of target-setting

■ Keep a register on a daily basis using the following codes:

✓ card/booklet completed as required

I card/booklet incomplete

M card/booklet missing

P no parental signature

A pupil absent

F pupil failed to appear for monitoring

■ If a pattern emerges of I, M, P or F, complete the *Area of Concern* form

■ If the pupil continues to fail to co-operate, once again complete the *Area of Concern Form* and a staged set of procedures should be invoked.

## Support Group Leader's Reflective Diary

This record (see example below and included on the CD Rom) is useful from several perspectives:

- it provides an accurate record of work taking place within the groups

- it helps the Support Group Leader to reflect upon his/her practice and to learn from it

- in schools in which there is more than one group operating, the records can provide an overview of practice and serve as a focus for the evaluation and sharing of good practice.

## Example of Support Group Leaders' Reflective Diary

| Date | Activities | Aspects which worked well | Aspects which could be improved |
|------|-----------|--------------------------|-------------------------------|
|      |           |                          |                               |
|      |           |                          |                               |

## Support Group lesson plans and materials

The programme has been devised around the Teaching for Understanding Framework, as described in Chapter 4. As such, the following terminology is used within the Activity Guides: generative topics, understanding goals, understanding performances and ongoing assessment. The activities are classified according to Generative Topics as follows:

| | |
|---|---|
| Introductory | An introduction to the approach and its aims, target-setting, the Support Group Pledge and the Support Group Diary |
| Section 1 | The dynamic of the classroom context and the nature of relationships within it |
| Section 2 | A focus upon learning, upon the factors which dispose pupils towards learning or act as impediments to it and the purpose of schooling |
| Section 3 | A focus upon self-esteem, the motivations which underlie behaviour, self-control and self-responsibility |
| Section 4 | A focus upon moral values and upon peer relationships |
| Plenary | Reflecting upon what has been learned within the groups |

With the exceptions of the introductory set of lessons and the plenary session, the sections can be undertaken in any order, although it is not advised that groups 'dip in and out' of sections as a coherent approach is required. It is also advised that the activities within each section are undertaken in the order in which they are presented. An overview of the programme as a whole is provided below.

## Programme for Support Groups

### Programme Overview

| Section | Act | Focus of activity | Recommended time |
|---|---|---|---|
| Int: The context of the Support Group | Int 1a-c | Understanding the aims and nature of the group | 3+ sessions (follow lesson guidelines) |
| 1: The classroom situation | Act 1a<br>Act 1b<br>Act 1c | Understanding different perspectives<br>Conceptions of behaviour<br>Values and beliefs | 1 session<br>1 session<br>2+ sessions |
| 2: A focus upon learning | Act 2a<br>Act 2b<br>Act 2c<br>Act 2d<br>Act 2e | Factors that foster or inhibit learning<br>Factors over which pupils can exercise control<br>The beliefs that underlie learning<br>The purpose of education<br>Designing your ideal school | 1+ session<br>1+ session<br>1 session<br>1+ session<br>2 sessions |
| 3: A focus upon behaviour | Act 3a<br>Act 3b<br>Act 3c–d | Understanding motivation<br>Understanding stress reactions<br>Setting goals | 2 sessions<br>1 session<br>1 session |
| 4: Inter-personal relationships | Act 4a<br><br>Act 4b<br>Act 4c | Moral dilemmas in the context of relationships<br>Bullying scenario<br>Reflecting upon bullying | 2 sessions<br><br>1 + session<br>1 session |
| 5: Reflecting upon learning | Plenary | What have I learned? How have I changed?<br>Individual interviews arranged with each pupil | 1 session<br>30–40 mins per pupil |

It is important to recognise that activities (with the exception of the introductory and plenary sections) do not correspond to lessons; they take as long as is required for them to be adequately explored (the timings given above are for guidance only). The format of each session (50–60 min) should include time for the target-setting process. The Understanding Goals as set out for each activity, should be shared with pupils, in user-friendly language, at the beginning of each session. The Support Group Diary should be used in a flexible manner, as described in Chapter 2.

Detailed teachers' guidelines take two forms:

- a section outline, which sets out the Generative Topic, Understanding Goals, Understanding Performances and Ongoing Assessment for each section (see, for example, Support Group Leaders' Guide to Activities: Section 1).

- an outline for each activity/lesson, which sets out the underlying goals, the thinking skills that should be generated within each activity, the materials required (and information regarding their organisation) and methodology (see, for example, Support Group Leaders' Guide to Activities: Activity 1c).

The pupil materials (exemplified on pp. 72–77) encompass:

- activity sheets

- information sheets

- charts and templates for completion

- card-sorts.

Pupil activities are not worksheets for pupils to work through on their own (nor are they designed for whole class use) and the SG Leader should read through the activities with the pupils, providing further explanation when required. Questions on the activity sheets and information sheets are intended as prompts for discussion, not questions to be answered in writing. If pupils are asked to respond in writing, this will be made clear in the Support Group Leaders' Guide to Activities, and the guidelines should be referred to prior to introducing any activity. Differentiation is achieved through the individual interactions between the Support Group Leader and pupils.

## Example: three of 18 cards for Activity 1c – values and beliefs

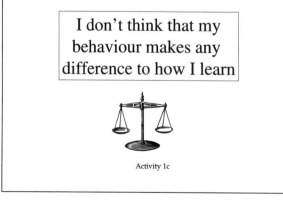

## Example: Activity 1c – values and beliefs

---

# Values and Beliefs

| Activity 1c |
| --- |

Not Certain

Disagree

Agree

❏ Take the set of cards and sort them into three bundles: agree, disagree or not certain. This exercise <u>must be done on your own</u> with no discussion with any other pupils.

❏ Write a code at the back of each card as follows:
A    agree
NC   not certain
D    disagree

❏ Place your cards onto the chart depending upon the choices you made.

❏ Your Support Group Leader will ask one of you to select a card. You will tell the group where you placed the card.

❏ The Support Group Leader will then go round the group asking where other pupils have placed the same card.

❏ The Support Group Leader will then open the discussion by asking each of you to explain why you placed the card as you did. You should all become involved in the discussion, asking questions of each other.

❏ When you have finished with a card you should hand it over to the Support Group Leader to be kept apart from the other cards.

❏ Now repeat the last four steps until all of the cards have been discussed.

**Example: Worksheet for Activity 3a – understanding motivation**

# Motivation

| Activity 3a |
| --- |

❑ Choose a situation which has recently taken place in which you felt stressed – perhaps a situation in which there was an argument between yourself and another person.

❑ Go through the situation with your Support Group Leader and identify the things which you believe you gained from the situation and the things which you lost from it. Think about it not only from your own point of view but also the effects upon others.

❑ As you each discuss your own situations, other members of the group can contribute helpful comments and questions.

❑ When you have completed the exercise and your Support Group Leader has helped you each to complete the chart, answer the question at the bottom, with the help of the Support Group Leader and the other pupils in the group.

Gains

❑

❑

❑

❑

❑

Losses

❑

❑

❑

❑

❑

What would you do differently if you were in the same situation again?

**Example: Information Sheets 9a and 9b – 'The Fight or Flight Response'**

---

## Stress Reactions

*The Fight or Flight Response*

Physical Changes in the Body

❑ Blood vessels tighten resulting in a rise of blood pressure

❑ Blood flow increases to where it is needed (the heart) and away from the skin and digestive system

❑ There is a rise in adrenalin (to help us to run) and cortisol (to cope with pain)

Information Sheet 9a

---

## Stress Reactions

*The Fight or Flight Response*

Brain Responses

When a person feels stressed, instead of a signal going to the part of the brain which controls thinking, it goes directly to the part of the brain which causes the physical changes in the body (sheet 9a) and to the amygdala which controls the emotions. This results in people acting without thinking.

Information Sheet 9b

## Example: Pupil worksheet for Activity 4b – bullying scenario

| Activity 4b |
| --- |

Angela has fallen out with her best friend, Alison. It started when Alison 'made up to' Angela's boyfriend at a party. Angela and Alison aren't speaking to each other apart from to call each other names. Angela's friends, Jane and Lorna, have also started to call Alison names and to talk about her behind her back.

No one will speak to Alison in the class or sit with her at lunchtime. Margaret and Laura don't like what's happening to Alison but they're too frightened to do anything about it in case the others start to pick on them. Jane and Lorna pass a message to Alison to say that Angela wants to fight with her. Alison doesn't want to get in a fight but her Mum and Dad have always told her to stick up for herself – give as good as she gets.

Margaret and Laura tell the class teacher about the bullying. She says that it will pass over – girls are always falling in and out. There is no clear policy in the school about bullying 'there's no problem here!'. However, one of the other teachers hears some pupils in the class talking about the proposed fight and tells the Depute Head Teacher. He has a class at the time and doesn't have time to deal with the matter until the bell rings at lunchtime. He looks for the girls but can't find them.

At lunchtime, a big crowd of pupils gather around Angela and Alison. Alison gets frightened and tries to push off Angela. Angela turns on her and punches her. It turns into a big fight and both girls are sent home with a letter of suspension. Alison is frightened of how her parents might react and runs away from home.

- ❑ Working together as a group, decide who is most at fault in this situation. Use the cards provided and place them on the grid.

- ❑ Is this a case of bullying or is it just two girls falling out? Explain your answer.

- ❑ Is it always the case that there is a 'baddie' and a 'goodie' in situations like this?

- ❑ Take each person or group of people in turn and describe how things could have been handled differently to avoid the situation getting worse.

- ❑ In which way(s) might the school's systems (its ways of dealing with things) be at fault. How would you improve things?

# Example: worksheet for Activity 4b – bullying scenario

| Activity 4b |
| --- |

- ❑ Read over the story.

- ❑ Working together as a group, take each card in turn and place them in order as described below according to the part they played in the situation.

- ❑ Return to the sheet and complete the remaining activities/questions.

## Who's to blame

| Most at fault |
| --- |

| | |
| --- | --- |

| | | |
| --- | --- | --- |

| | |
| --- | --- |

| Least at fault |
| --- |

# Assessment of pupil outcomes

Advice relating to the evaluation of Support Groups is provided in Chapter 8, but clearly any evaluation needs to be informed by evidence relating to the extent to which pupils have attained the desired outcomes as set out in Chapter 3. Assessing pupil outcomes in relation to the affective domain is a much more complex and demanding task than assessing progress in academic fields and requires triangulation in approach, that is, drawing from a range of different sources of evidence by a range of means.

Whilst there is a tendency to assume that 'hard indicators' (for example, examination results, attendance statistics) are a much more reliable indicator than personal accounts, this is not necessarily the case. It is hard to 'tell the story' behind statistics – why a child might attain poor results or have poor attendance. Personal accounts provide a depth of insight which can illuminate the hard data. Likewise, some pupil outcomes may take time to be realised and perhaps it is more important to look for indicators of future improvement (for example, a pupil who has developed learning habits such as asking for help and persevering when in difficulty). An approach that draws from a range of evidence, bringing together quantitative data (for example, statistics) and qualitative data (for example, personal accounts attained through interview or open-questionnaires which allow for a more in-depth response) is most likely to provide an accurate picture.

In the following pages, a checklist cross-referencing the aims of the Support Group to sources of evidence is provided (see 'Support Group Evaluation Checklist', p. 79) followed by examples of evaluation tools (questionnaires, interview schedules) (see pp. 80, 81). Detailed guidance is provided on the CD Rom for the conduct of such tools. The full range of research tools is set out below.

## Evaluation tools

| Stakeholder | Research tool |
| --- | --- |
| Pupils | Self-evaluation pre-intervention questionnaire (Likert scale) Self-evaluation post-intervention questionnaire (Likert scale) Interview (based upon interview schedule) |
| Class teachers | Open- and closed-response questionnaire |
| Parents | Open- and closed-response questionnaire |

## Support Group Evaluation Checklist

| Support Group aims | Evidence in support of Aims |
|---|---|
| Pupils gain insight into their attitudes (thoughts and feelings), values, beliefs and motivations and those of others | 1. pupils' participation in group discussion<br>2. pupils' discussions of their diaries<br>3. the selection and evaluation of targets<br>4. pupils' responses to the self-assessment: 'What have I learned?' and Likert scale questionnaire<br>5. pupils' responses to the interview with SG Leaders<br>6. parents' responses to the questionnaire |
| Pupils develop further their capacity to self-regulate their behaviour through applying what they have learned with good judgement to other contexts | 1. pupils' conduct within the group – are they able to exercise self-control?<br>2. pupils' conduct in classes and around the school<br>3. a reduction in the number and severity of indiscipline measures (e.g. detentions, referrals, suspensions)<br>4. class teachers' responses on target cards<br>5. class teachers' responses to the questionnaire<br>6. pupils' responses to the self-assessment: 'How have I changed?' and to the Likert scale questionnaire<br>7. pupils' responses to the interview with Sg Leaders<br>8. parents' responses to the questionnaire |
| Pupils develop further their capacity for empathy and the quality of their inter-personal relationships | 1. pupils in group discussion demonstrate a greater capacity to consider perspectives other than their own and to show consideration to others<br>2. pupils behave with greater consideration towards others in classes and around the school<br>3. as for 3–8 above |
| Pupils develop further their self-esteem and confidence | 1. pupils, through their general conduct, appear to be more relaxed and comfortable in their inter-personal relationships<br>2. pupils appear to be more willing and able to contribute meaningfully to group discussion and to participate in activities<br>3. as for 3–8 above |
| Pupils develop more positive learning dispositions and more positive attitudes towards school. | 1. pupils participate more actively in their learning and take greater responsibility for it (e.g. completion of homework tasks; coming to school equipped for lessons)<br>2. pupils are developing a range of strategies which enable them to learn more effectively (e.g. asking for help when required; forward planning)<br>3. pupils are more positive in their attitudes towards school and are more aware of its purpose<br>4. improved attendance and reduced truancy<br>5. as for 3–8 above. |

# Pre-intervention assessment form

Tick one box only for each statement
Please respond to every statement.

| Positive Statements | | | | Negative Statements |
|---|---|---|---|---|
| I understand my behaviour | | | | I don't understand my behaviour |
| I behave well in school | | | | I don't behave well in school |
| I am happy and relaxed about how I behave | | | | I am unhappy and anxious about how I behave |
| I can control my behaviour when I want to | | | | I can't control my behaviour when I want to |
| I can control my temper when under pressures | | | | I lose my temper when under pressure |
| I want to improve upon my behaviour | | | | I don't want to improve upon my behaviour |
| I am concerned about how my behaviour affects others | | | | I am not concerned about how my behaviour affects others |
| I make friends easily | | | | I don't make friends easily |
| I get on well with my friends | | | | I frequently fall out with my friends |
| I am usually friendly towards other pupils | | | | I am often aggressive towards others pupils |
| Other pupils are usually friendly towards me | | | | Other pupils are usually aggressive towards me |
| I get on well with my teachers | | | | I don't get on well with my teachers |
| Most of my teachers like me | | | | Most of my teachers don't like me |
| Most of my teachers are fair | | | | Most of my teachers are not fair |
| I try to show respect towards my teachers | | | | I don't treat teachers with respect |
| Most of my teachers treat me with respect | | | | Most of my teachers don't treat me with respect |
| I can talk to some of my teachers | | | | I can't talk to any of my teachers |
| Most of my teachers care about me | | | | Most of my teachers don't care about me |
| I feel good about myself most of the time | | | | I don't feel good about myself most of the time |
| I think of myself as being quite intelligent | | | | I think that I'm stupid |
| I consider myself to be a good learner | | | | I don't consider myself to be a good learner |
| I can work at a problem until I get it right | | | | I give up when I have difficulty |
| I ask for help when I get stuck | | | | I don't ask for help when I get stuck |
| I like school | | | | I don't like school |

Name:                                                    Date:

# Example: Pupil interview schedule (page 1 of three)

## Pupil Interview

As a result of participating within a Support Group has there been any change in:

| Questions | Prompts | Responses |
|---|---|---|
| your understanding of yourself?<br><br>*Why do you think that?*<br>*Tell me more*<br>*Can you give me an e.g.?* | ☐ your feelings<br>☐ what you believe in<br>☐ what you think is important<br>☐ what motivates you to want to do things | |
| your understanding of other people?<br><br>*Why do you think that?*<br>*Tell me more*<br>*Can you give me an e.g.?* | ☐ how they feel<br>☐ what they believe in<br>☐ what they think is important<br>☐ what motivates them to want to do things | |
| your ability to control your behaviour?<br><br><br><br><br><br>*Why do you think that?*<br>*Tell me more*<br>*Can you give me an e.g.?* | ☐ being able to behave appropriately in classes and around the school<br>☐ being able to control your temper<br>☐ being able to take responsibility for your behaviour (e.g. saying sorry) | |
| your ability to listen to and take account of other people's views?<br><br>*Why do you think that?*<br>*Tell me more*<br>*Can you give me an e.g.?* | ☐ being able to contribute effectively to group and class discussions<br>☐ being able to respond in a mature way to what is said to you | |

In the plenary session prior to the individual interviews conducted by the Support Group Leader (for which time needs to be put aside), pupils are encouraged to reflect upon their learning by answering the following questions and by completing the post-intervention self-assessment questionnaire (see CD Rom):

- What have I learned about me?

  - my values

  - my beliefs

  - my attitudes

  - my motivations

- What have I learned about my relationships with others?

- Have I changed:

  - in my relationships with others?

  - in my ability to control my behaviour and take responsibility for it?

  - in self-esteem and confidence?

  - in my attitudes towards learning and school and my learning habits?

**Summary**

This chapter has described the day-to-day management of Support Groups and provided a range of examples of Support Group materials, including the Support Group Leaders' Guide to Activities. Guidance is provided relating to the assessment of pupil outcomes, including the identification of evidence in support of findings.

Examples of research tools are also given. It is important that this chapter is read/used in conjunction with the advice and guidance provided throughout the book and on the CD Rom.

# THE WIDER PICTURE

# Implementing and Sustaining Support Groups at Whole-School Level

> This chapter brings together the themes from the previous chapters and looks at how Support Groups can be integrated into school policy and practice such that they can be sustainable. The chapter discusses:
>
> ➤ the nature of the change process – factors that can facilitate or act as impediments to change
> ➤ staff development and the management of groups
> ➤ monitoring and evaluation of the initiative.

## Managing change

As a senior manager in two Secondary schools spanning a nine-year period, I became very aware of the challenges (and frustrations) inherent in managing change. Schools are being bombarded on all sides by initiatives, directives and targets, which, if taken in isolation, may be very worthy but which, if taken together, lead to a sense of overload over which it is hard for managers and teachers to have any coherent overview or sense of ownership. In order to succeed, one needs to take account not only of the initiative itself but the environment in which it is to be embedded.

Michael Fullan (2003) argues that the change process is highly complex and, if change is to be sustainable, certain conditions need to prevail. The chapter draws upon these conditions and relates them to Support Group work.

### Coping with uncertainty

Embarking upon any new initiative can be a difficult experience for individuals (whether staff, parents or pupils) as it often means that people have to move beyond their 'comfort zones', to embrace uncertainty. Chapter 6 explored in detail the role of the Support Group Leader and how this differs from the more traditional roles teachers play within schools. If well supported by an effective infra-structure (including high quality staff development) and within a setting in which strong foundations for the initiative to develop have been built, much of this uncertainty can be alleviated. Likewise, if careful steps are taken to communicate effectively with pupils and parents and to consult with them about participation within the Support Group Initiative (SGI), many of the fears parents and pupils initially hold can be allayed and problems encountered on the way can be dealt with promptly before they escalate.

## The process of meaning-making and the creation of a climate that promotes and sustains change

The emphasis upon the philosophy and influences underlying the SGI within this text is to enable teachers to 'make meaning' of the approach not only for themselves but for their pupils, to 'make their own connections' (which may be applicable to other aspects of their practice) and, through this process of meaning-making, to internalise the ideas, values and beliefs which underlie the approach. Real, sustainable, change is about reaching out to the 'hearts and minds' of individuals, which can only be achieved if people are enabled to engage at a deeper level with the underlying ideas and to relate them to their own set of circumstances. Therefore, it is important that in putting the SGI into practice teachers are encouraged to engage with these concepts at all stages of implementation, an important aspect of staff development.

However, this process of meaning-making is not only important for those most directly involved in the initiative but also for the wider school community. All staff, parents and pupils within the school should be made aware of the development of the approach within the school and its aims, with the opportunity provided for discussion. An inclusive and open approach is much less likely to lead to stigmatisation of pupils, and parents are often re-assured that the school is taking a pro-active approach in supporting pupils and minimising disruption.

Chapter 5 argued that Support Groups should not be seen as an 'add-on' to the school but as an integral part of the pastoral care services provided by the school for its pupils and as part of the inter-disciplinary approach, involving a range of agencies, to support young people and their families. It is important therefore to consider the ways in which Support Groups can complement and enhance current provision. As suggested in Chapter 1, it is desirable that Support Groups should become part of the annual development planning process within the school.

## The reasons why teachers may reject innovations

It can be anticipated, however, that there may be pockets of resistance to the development of the approach. Whilst it is easy to be dismissive of teachers who appear to be 'set in their ways', it is important to understand why this might be the case. Teachers who have been sufficiently long in post to see variations of past practice in 'new clothing' or who have been at the receiving end of innovations that appear to be 'flavour of the month' and are not followed through as other more 'inviting' innovations come over the horizon are right to be sceptical. These teachers cannot be browbeaten into submission and nor should they be. They have experience that can be drawn upon and they should be listened to and encouraged to express their reservations, as it is only through open discussion that understanding on both sides can develop.

If one also considers the serious reservations expressed by teachers about inclusion (and in particular, the presumption of mainstreaming of pupils with SEBD), as discussed in Chapter 5, and the feelings expressed by some teachers that pupils with behavioural difficulties are not deserving of support (often expressed in terms of 'They get too much attention already. What about the well-behaved kids?'), it is likely that some of these teachers will be resistant.

Other teachers reject innovations on moral or ethical grounds or on the basis that they do not believe that the innovations are in the best interests of their pupils. For example, there are some who would reject approaches such as Support Groups on the basis that such approaches, to them, promote a 'deficit model' of the child (the child 'needs fixing'), arguing instead for a focus upon systems and practice. It should be recognised that, in providing additional support to children, the school is adapting its practice. An inclusive ethos cannot be legislated for – it has to come from within the hearts and minds of all of the school community and an understanding of the change process would lead one to the conclusion that in order to change the environment one has to initially put in place small changes which encourage people to question their values and beliefs and to look at situations from a new perspective. Fullan (2003) draws from the work of Gladwell (2000), who identifies the concept of the 'tipping point' ('little causes can have big effects'), to note the importance of context as an agent of change when groups model new behaviour, creating a new context. Gladwell states:

> If you want ... to bring about a fundamental change in people's belief and behavior, a change that would persist and serve as an example to others, you need to create a community around them, where these new beliefs could be practiced, expressed and nurtured. (Gladwell, 2000: 173)

It is often only retrospectively that one can recognise when the 'tipping point' in any initiative has been reached. It occurs at the point at which the new beliefs and values become internalised by the group and begin to become part of the 'norms' of the institution, part of the ethos and culture.

## The 'tipping point'

This is indeed the approach we adopted within the school. A defining moment for me came at a presentation to Pastoral Care staff (where it was clear that the over-riding feeling was, 'What does this mean for my workload?') when one of the teachers said, 'Hold on a minute. Three of my pupils were in Joan's group last year and they were unrecognisable at the end of the year.' At that point, other staff started to come on board and the approach never looked back.

Likewise, the initial lukewarm response of some staff to Support Groups was entirely transformed over time when the response to the in-service training day (seven years after initial implementation) was, 'Why don't we have more groups?', 'Should we not start earlier?', 'How can we extend the groups beyond S2?'. Thus, the environment became inclusive not because the staff were told that they should become more inclusive in their practice but because they had internalised the values of the approach and had seen the changes in individual pupils.

Effective management of change takes time, patience, humility, perseverance, problem-solving capacities, a willingness to listen and embrace new ideas, and flexibility and responsiveness in approach. If one strategy does not succeed, try another. Being sensitive to the environment, being aware of those staff members who are influential, who can act as a force for good and who can help to take things forward is an important aspect in effecting change. There are important messages to be learned from this.

**Reflection Point**

Reflecting back upon successful innovations that have occurred within your school or within your classroom (e.g. the introduction of a new policy or teaching methodology), can you identify a 'tipping point' – a point at which people began to come on board and embrace the new ideas and changes? What changes led to that point and how were they achieved?

## Creating communities of practice

Gladwell's identification of the need to create a community of practice in which new beliefs can be expressed and nurtured is an important element in effecting sustainable change. Communities of practice are identified by Wenger et al. as being:

> Groups of people who share a concern, a set of problems, or a passion about a topic, and who deepen their knowledge and expertise in this area by interacting on an ongoing basis. (Wenger et al., 2002: 4 in Fullan, 2003: 45)

A community of practice is dependent upon people having a shared common purpose with which they can each identify. However, Fullan does not just identify purpose as being important but *moral* purpose. If change is not directed towards good, would we wish it to be sustainable? Experienced and successful leaders will know that this common purpose can only lead to effective and sustainable change through working with and through others. Fullan makes the case for leadership not to be invested solely in one individual (the 'charismatic headteacher') or even in a group of individuals (the Senior Management Team) but to be distributed throughout the school. He does not make this argument on the basis of egalitarian notions but on the basis that the strength of an institution rests on the strengths of all of its members. If change is to be sustainable it is imperative that the community has knowledge and understanding and the range of skills to be able to carry forward and transform initiatives even beyond their initial conceptualisations. This is not to say that there is not a need for a clearly identified project leader and team to support that leader. The argument I am forwarding is that the leader should be investing in the capabilities of all within the community (staff, parents and pupils) in order to build capacity. This is not just a theoretical position but a practical one. The model I am proposing to develop the infra-structure to support the SGI is dependent upon the concept of distributed leadership, with staff collaborating to learn from each other and to support each other – a true community of learners.

As this stands, it is a fine principle but how is it to be achieved? There are several components that I would consider to be essential:

- the leader needs to be willing to explore new ideas with an open mind and to reach outwards to embrace new thinking

- the leader needs to enable others to do likewise and to provide opportunities for the sharing of ideas and reflection upon them (not an easy undertaking in busy schools but, if considered a priority, it can be done)

- a shared vision needs to develop through open communication and consultation, leading to the establishment of clear aims and objectives

- the leader needs to create the infra-structure to support the development of new initiatives – resources, staff training and development, networking and the development of communication channels – seeking the support of school governors/parent council and the LEA (if required)

■ the leader, through acquiring insight into the strengths and development needs of staff, must identify opportunities through which staff can develop their leadership skills (e.g. taking forward aspects of the project)

■ ongoing monitoring is essential, in conjunction with a responsive and adaptable approach

■ an improvement cycle be implemented, in which evaluation leads to the identification of action points.

**Reflection Point**

If you were to give consideration to introducing Support Groups to your school, what would you see as the existing strengths of your school which would facilitate implementation (for example, enthusiastic individuals on the staff who have the right qualities and experience to take the project forward)? What might the impediments to change be? How can you build upon the strengths and address the difficulties? How would you go about planning for implementation?

## Staff development and the management of Support Groups

There has been a tendency to equate staff development with in-service training delivered by 'experts' and to under-estimate the strengths and capabilities of people within the school, but it should be clear from the previous section that a much broader conception is being put forward, one that embraces all activities in which people participate that serve to enhance their own professional knowledge, understanding and skills and those of others. Thus, in relation to Support Groups, it could embrace a wide range of activities, including:

■ formal in-service training

■ role-play

■ personal reading followed by 'pair and share'

■ the development of knowledge, understanding and skills 'in situ' through observing and assisting with or leading a Support Group and the process of critical reflection upon one's own practice

■ providing support to others through mentoring or team-teaching or sharing insights gained through one's own professional development

■ developing one's communication skills through building up partnerships with parents, other staff and (if appropriate to the post held within the school) external agencies such as psychological services and social work

■ the sharing of good practice and collaborative problem-solving in Support Group Leader meetings

■ the opportunity to develop further, materials and evaluation tools suited to the needs of one's own pupils.

This text and the materials on the CD Rom (including a Powerpoint presentation for staff on key aspects of the approach) should serve as a tool in the development of staff. Chapter 2 outlined the range of mechanisms that are employed in relation to staff development, and the role of the project leader is crucial in ensuring that a high quality of support is provided to Support Group Leaders. Likewise, both Chapters 2 and 5 and the initial section of this chapter have highlighted the importance of staff training for the whole staff, as they will be involved in the day-to-day encounters with Support Group pupils and in the target-setting process.

In the initial stages it may be advisable to involve two members of staff in leading the group until staff confidence and skills develop. It is important that the Project Leader should initially be involved in leading a group as otherwise he or she will lack the insight to be able to act as an effective role-model for others and to be able to advise others effectively. One of the most important aspects of effective leadership is to lead from the front and it was always my maxim not to ask someone to undertake something I was not prepared to do myself. Good leaders are always willing to 'go that extra mile'. The 'cascade' model through which people who gain experience act as mentors for others and support them in the initial stages through team-teaching has proved to be highly effective and helps to 'cement' the team and create the sense of community to which reference has previously been made.

The Project Leader should also act as a liaison between senior management and the team, negotiating time for staff development and meetings. As discussed in Chapter 1, the Project Leader also negotiates the means by which staff are enabled to lead groups. Whilst it was regarded as a voluntary activity within the school, which was not counted against class contact time, it was noted that staff were involved and, where possible, it was set against the time when they might be called upon to cover classes for absent colleagues.

---

**Action Point**

After having read the advice given and having perused the materials relating to staff development on the CD Rom, begin to devise an initial plan which could form the basis of taking this area forward and discuss it with colleagues. Give consideration to the focus of each input, the form that it should take, the resources required and the people who would be responsible. Remember that a range of different approaches should be adopted.

---

## Monitoring and evaluation

### How do we measure, or place a value on 'Linda smiled this year'?

There is a tendency to assume that because an intervention is well intentioned that it 'works', yet, how often do schools thoroughly evaluate initiatives which are put in place? Are we aware of the effects on individuals, on the ethos of the school and upon the wider community of our actions? Yet, on the other hand, in the quest for accountability there is a focus upon things that are easy to measure (examination results, attendance data etc.) at the expense of things that are less definable, such as the mental health and well-being of our young people. The narrow focus upon targets and upon league tables has fostered a climate in which young people get lost within the system and are deemed to be of less worth if they do not contribute positively towards these outcomes.

The focus has gradually shifted in schools throughout the UK from one of external evaluation to one of school self-evaluation (verified by external inspection), as set out in *A New Relationship with*

*Schools: Improving Performance through School Evaluation* (DfES, 2005b)/ *How Good is our School?*, rev. edn (HMIE, 2002b) and its most recent manifestation, *The Journey to Excellence* (HMIE, 2006b).

MacBeath and McGlynn (2002) set out a case for school self-evaluation, focusing on the school as a learning community. They argue that the primary concern has to do with 'what happens in individual classrooms, with individual teachers and with individual learners' (MacBeath and McGlynn, 2002: 6). They believe that self-evaluation should not concern itself solely with easy to measure performance but with reflecting upon how the school learns and what it can do to improve its performance and to build capacity for learning.

The evaluation of performance is not an end-on to be thought about at the end of the intervention. The criteria upon which it should be based and the means by which it should be carried out should be established at the initial planning and development stages. Establishing clear aims and objectives is essential as it is only possible to know if one has been successful when one knows what one is setting out to achieve. In the case of Support Groups, the criteria for success are set out within the research aims and questions (see Chapter 3) which, in turn, reflect the aims of the approach. Just as a case has been made for Support Groups to be perceived as integral to the school, likewise the success criteria should reflect the aims of the school, which in turn should reflect LEA and national priorities – we should all be singing from the same hymn sheet!

---

**Reflection Point**

To what extent are staff aware in your school of the aims and objectives of the school and of those of the LEA and UK Government/Scottish Executive? Are staff familiar with the five outcomes of *Every Child Matters* (UK)/the National Priorities and four elements of *A Curriculum for Excellence* and ten dimensions of *The Journey to Excellence* (Scotland)?

When was the last time your school re-visited its aims and objectives in line with national initiatives? To what extent are the whole-school staff involved in the process or is it a task undertaken by senior management? What is more important – the product or the process?

---

School leaders and classroom teachers are often so busy in the 'day-to-day' business of the school that it is often very difficult for them to raise their heads above the parapet, and perhaps there is an important message for government within this observation. The school needs to adopt a whole-school approach towards evaluation, providing guidance to departments and staff, and ensuring that staff are familiar with the guidance given in national documentation. The basic questions set out in *A New Relationship …* (DfES, 2005b)/*HGIOS* (HMIE, 2002b) provide a simple framework around which evaluation can be organised (see p. 92). These questions put an onus on schools to identify an evidence base upon which they can draw to justify their conclusions and to identify action points that can lead to further improvement.

The questions are expanded upon further within the OFSTED document that focuses principally upon the processes of effective self-evaluation, whereas the more recent Scottish document *The Journey to Excellence* (HMIE, 2006b) focuses more upon outcomes:

- What have we achieved?

- How well do we meet the needs of our school community?

- How good is the education we provide?

- How good is our management?

- How good is our leadership?

- What is our capacity for improvement? (HMIE, 2006b:25)

## Framework for evaluation

| UK Government | Scottish Executive |
|---|---|
| How well are we doing?<br><br>How can we do better?<br><br>(DfES, 2005b) | How are we doing?<br><br>How do we know?<br><br>What are we going to do now?<br><br>(HMIE, 2002b) |

In the UK context, more detailed guidance in relation to outcomes is provided in the advice given by OFSTED to LEAs and schools in relation to the Joint Area Reviews of children's services (OFSTED, 2005), focusing upon *Every Child Matters*.

Chapter 7 sets out some of the tools that are used within the Support Group to evaluate the progress of individual pupils, which serves the function not only of being able to provide feedback to the child, class teachers and parents but which, when taken collectively, enable an overview of progress to be formed. Whilst within the research study a wide range of data was gathered, including statistics relating to attendance, truancy, attainment and measures of indiscipline, it is not advocated that such an in-depth approach is adopted, although it may be of value to track individual progress in relation to indiscipline measures such as referrals to senior management and suspensions from school. There are simple mechanisms that can be adopted to evaluate progress, such as the completion of the Support Group Leader's Reflective Diary (see Chapter 7), which can then used as the basis of discussion at Support Group Leaders' meetings.

On-going informal monitoring of progress through discussion at Support Group Leaders' meetings, discussions with pupils of their target-cards and reflective diaries, the regular 'pop-in' visits of experienced Support Group Leaders to groups, and the regular communication with parents and class teachers through the target-setting process are all means of gathering information that will inform decision-making. The more formal mechanisms (as set out in Chapter 7) are all sources of valuable information which inform the reports sent home to parents. However, if the information to be obtained is to be regarded as reliable, it is important that criteria are set out for the conduct, analysis and reporting of each and that staff receive training (see guidance on the CD Rom for Support Group Leaders implementing evaluation tools).

However, the most important mechanism is the discussion that takes place at the end of each session amongst Support Group Leaders when staff, drawing upon all of the evidence available to them (as described above) are asked to identify the strengths and weaknesses (areas for development) of the approach as a means of identifying priorities which then feed into the development plan for the following session. This is identical to the process advocated in the guidelines provided by OFSTED in relation to self-evaluation (DfES, 2005b: 5). A template to assist with this process is provided on the CD Rom, with an extract at the end of the chapter (see 94).

This chapter concludes with extracts from a checklist and template developed around the ten dimensions of *The Journey to Excellence* (see CD Rom), which provides a framework that, whilst related directly to the Scottish context, is also highly applicable to the UK as a whole and which is cross-referenced to the five outcomes of *Every Child Matters* [ECM] (DfES, 2004a):

| *Every Child Matters* | Ref |
|---|---|
| Be healthy | ECM 1 |
| Stay safe | ECM 2 |
| Enjoy and achieve | ECM 3 |
| Make a positive contribution | ECM 4 |
| Achieve economic well-being | ECM 5 |

The checklist can serve two purposes – in the planning and implementation stage of the project and in the evaluation stage. A summary of the processes that apply to all stakeholders in relation to Support Groups is provided on the CD Rom.

## Extract from checklist for Support Group evaluation (dimension 1 of ten)

---

*Support Group evalution*

1: *Engages young people in the highest quality learning activities (ECM 3, 4 & 5)*

✓  learning is relevant and meaningful to the lives of young people

✓  pupils participate actively in group activities

✓  pupils participate actively in the target-setting process

✓  pupils are encouraged to take responsibility for their own learning

✓  pupils are encouraged to reflect upon their learning

✓  thinking skills are promoted through group activities

✓  the learning takes account of the starting point of individual pupils

✓  pupils receive appropriate support and challenge

**Illustration of template for Support Group evaluation based on the ten dimensions of *The Journey to Excellence* (and five outcomes of *Every Child Matters*)**

## Support Group Evaluation

| Dimension | Strengths | Development Needs |
|---|---|---|
| Engages young people in the highest quality learning activities (*ECM* 3, 4 & 5) | | |
| Focuses on outcomes and maximises success for all learners (*ECM* 1–5) | | |
| Develops a common vision across children and young people, parents and staff (*ECM* 4 & 5) | | |
| Fosters high quality leadership at all levels (*ECM* 5) | | |
| Works in partnership with other agencies and its community (*ECM* 1, 2 & 5) | | |

| Dimension | Strengths | Development Needs |
|---|---|---|
| Works together with parents to promote learning (*ECM* 3, 4 & 5) | | |
| Reflects on its own work and thrives on challenge (*ECM* 5) | | |
| Values and empowers its staff and young people (*ECM* 3, 4 & 5) | | |
| Promotes well-being and respect (*ECM* 1–5) | | |
| Develops a culture of ambition and achievement (*ECM* 3–5) | | |

**Summary**

This chapter has explored the change process and the factors which can either foster or hinder effective change and sustainability, exploring such issues as the need to take account of the environment in which the change is to be embedded, to endeavour towards a sense of shared purpose and to work through others. The chapter has examined the range of mechanisms through which staff development can be fostered. It has also focused on the process of self-evaluation, suggesting that it should not be seen as an 'end-on' but as part of the integral planning process, arising from the clear identification of aims and objectives.

## CHAPTER 9

# The Implications of Support Group Work

This chapter focuses on:

➤ an overview of pupil progress
➤ the response of pupils and parents to the SGI
➤ the wider impact of the SGI within the school
➤ the variables that may affect pupil outcome
➤ the wider implications of Support Group work in relation to national initiatives and priorities

## Did Support Group pupils achieve the desired outcomes?

It is evident from examining the responses of a wide range of stakeholders, and from examination of data relating to attainment, attendance and indiscipline, that for the majority of Support Group pupils many of the desired outcomes that were expressed within the aims of the approach and reflected within the evaluative research questions had been achieved, to at least some extent and within some contexts. As would be expected, outcomes varied from pupil to pupil, and all pupils, even those for whom the outcomes were not so positive, gained something from participation within the initiative even if it was only a greater understanding of their difficulties. Whilst there is little evidence of improvements in attainment (and indeed the differentials between Support Group pupils and other pupils within the year group widened further) and attendance continued to deteriorate for both groups (a trend in line with national trends), the deterioration for Support Group pupils was less than that for other pupils within the year group and, indeed, whilst they had accounted for around half of all unauthorized absence in S1 (including exclusions from school), in S3 this had reduced to a third.

Indiscipline measures (referrals to senior management and days of suspension from school) reduced to a statistically highly significant extent (after having taken account of absence from school) for the Support Group pupils in the period after intervention, whilst they deteriorated to a highly significant extent for the other pupils within the group, taken as a whole.

This chapter explores the implications of the findings of the study in terms of understanding the variables that may affect pupil outcome and in relation to the wider picture – how the initiative can contribute towards imperatives such as social inclusion.

# The response of pupils and parents to the Support Group Initiative

It is clear from examining the response of pupils and parents that participation within the SGI was a positive experience for most pupils. Initial concerns about victimisation and stigmatisation were not realised. Whilst pupils' motivations for participation were variable – one pupil perceived it as an opportunity to *'get me out of German and avoid doing classwork'* – expectations from the perspective of parents and pupils were largely exceeded. In comparing the Support Group to a previous intervention, one pupil said, *'Here the teachers actually talk to you,'* and, further, *'Not what I expected. Not rubbish – turned out all right.'*

Pupils and parents appreciated the opportunity the groups provided for pupils to be able to discuss in an open and frank way, without fear of reprisals, their concerns, and this had led to the forming of more trusting and respectful relationships.

> *It worked because I was able to trust the people in the group.* (SG pupil)

It had helped to dissipate the anger some pupils felt towards school and their teachers and had enabled better partnership working between the home and the school.

> *Teachers are different and have different attitudes. I'm more able now to see teachers as individuals. I'm less angry than I used to be at teachers and at school in general. I can talk to some teachers now.* (SG pupil)

This boy's mother, in a letter of thanks, wrote of her son:

> *He is less frustrated and angry. He is more calm and definitely more confident in himself, definitely a much happier boy.*

## Does the effect last over time?

Without recourse to a much larger scale longitudinal study, it is difficult to state whether the effect of participation in a Support Group lasts over time. Within the boundaries of this study, pupils were followed for one or two years after intervention, checking upon their discipline and attendance records, requesting a report on their progress from the Depute Head Teacher responsible for S3, and a sample of pupils (around one-third) was interviewed retrospectively.

With the exception of one pupil, all pupils interviewed were unanimous in stating that involvement in the SGI had been of value to them. What became evident was that what pupils had derived from the initiative was personal to them, covering a wide range of outcomes.

> *I no longer need to be monitored. Can't remember when I last got a punishment exercise. Teachers treat me with more respect now. I'm quite confident I can keep it up. I have realised that these years are important now.* (SG pupil)

Not all outcomes were as positive, however.

## Case study: Linda

Linda's mother was very supportive of the school and very concerned about her daughter's behaviour. Linda had been moved to a new class at the beginning of S2 and had seemed to settle well but her Pastoral Care teacher was still concerned about her and nominated her for intervention. Linda, however, didn't consider that she needed help – 'teachers were picking on her'.

Linda's personal response to the group was mixed. She felt that she had gained some insight into her behaviour but this had not impacted upon it. This is reflected in her discipline record, which demonstrated a deteriorating pattern although her attainment was within normal parameters. There was a sharp deterioration in her behaviour and attendance in S3, the year after intervention. In retrospective interview, Linda expressed regret about the situation and was beginning to show signs of acknowledging her difficulties.

Linda's Support Group Leader felt that Linda's response to the group was disappointing. Linda might have derived more benefit if she had accepted responsibility for her behaviour rather than constantly justifying it. Responses of class teachers were very mixed, although some improvements were noted: 'Linda smiled this year'. There had been some improvements noted at home – 'Doesn't lose her temper so much' – but her mother felt that the group had not made a real difference to her daughter's behaviour – citing her daughter's inability to take responsibility for it.

(Based upon interviews conducted with Linda, her mother and SG Leader and class teacher questionnaires. Linda is a pseudonym).

Reports from the Depute Head responsible for S3 indicated that the majority of pupils were still experiencing difficulties in their behaviour as they progressed through the school but perhaps this is to be expected. The Behaviour Support teacher was quite clear that the effects of the group were often felt only after intervention. He noted the decreasing attendance at the Behaviour Support Base in subsequent years of pupils who had been involved in the SGI.

Given that the school is situated in one of the most deprived areas in Europe and that families in the community suffer from multiple deprivation, it is surprising that pupils respond positively at all given the odds against experiencing success. It is a community from which some young people descend into a life of crime and it may be the case that that will be the outcome for some of the youngsters who may have achieved a degree of success within the initiative, and it may be the case that others who have not responded so positively may blossom as other opportunities present to them in the future.

## The wider impact of the SGI within the school

Senior management were very supportive of the initiative and regarded it as a valuable adjunct to the approaches within the school to promote inclusion. It was clear that participation in the SGI had led some Support Group Leaders to re-evaluate their practice and to develop new ways of working, deepening their knowledge and understanding of pedagogy, introducing them to new ways of thinking about teaching and learning. It had led them to re-assess their relationships with pupils, seeing them in a new light. The view was expressed by some Pastoral Care teachers that it had enabled them to do what they had sought to achieve in becoming a Guidance teacher, away from the emphasis upon bureaucracy and paper-work.

But, perhaps even more importantly, did it impact upon the wider staff? This is a much harder question to answer. It was perhaps exemplified best through the way in which the approaches being advocated (such as target-setting) became part of the school's normal practice. It is true that some staff who were initially very cynical 'came on board' and were able to see changes in individual pupils, but this is certainly not the case for all staff and it is less clear that it impacted upon their practice within the classroom or in their relationships with individual pupils. However, it did lead to an understanding within the school that pupils with SEBD were as deserving of support as any other pupils with special/additional support needs.

# The variables that affect outcome

The findings should be interpreted with caution as the pupils' growing maturity may also be a factor in any improvement observed. (It should be noted, however, that pupils mostly attributed improvement to participation within the groups.) It was generally felt that participation in Support Groups had accelerated the process of maturation for pupils. Participation in other initiatives, such as the 'Toe-by-Toe' paired reading scheme and the activities of a charitable trust working within the community, and changes in family circumstances, could also have an impact upon pupil outcomes.

For those pupils experiencing the greatest difficulty in coping with school life, the combination of access to the Behaviour Support Base in conjunction with participation in a Support Group led by one of the Behaviour Support staff proved to be an effective solution; some of the most positive outcomes were recorded amongst these pupils (although this was not the case for all such pupils). It is clear that a multi-agency approach is desirable for many pupils but one of the difficulties in this respect is the demand upon resources, for example, the lengthy waiting times for appointments with Psychological Services.

## Did the groups always work well?

Given the target population for the groups, the majority of groups functioned very effectively indeed and I was often humbled at watching the Support Group Leaders in action, working with their pupils. However, even in groups that operated effectively most of the time, there were occasions when Support Group Leaders felt they had been 'put through the wringer', and I certainly had occasions when I wondered if I was achieving any good at all. This is when the value of regular Support Group Leader meetings come into play, when staff can act to support each other and a problem-solving approach can be adopted.

However, over the seven-year period and the forty or so groups that ran over that time, there were only one or two groups that proved to be dysfunctional, which were led by experienced Support Group Leaders who had led other successful groups. In each case, the groups were larger than normal (six pupils) and the 'mix' of pupils proved not to be conducive to successful group work. In one group, there were several pupils with ADHD and the solution we adopted was for me to team-teach with the Support Group Leader and to split the group.

## Are there any pupils for whom participation is not recommended?

A wide range of pupils, presenting with a range of different support needs, was involved within the SGI and it became evident that it was not possible to predict from previous records of indiscipline or attendance who would be likely to respond and who would not. Amongst those categorised initially as of 'low/some concern' (for whom it is not possible to demonstrate improvement in statistical terms), the majority demonstrated no deterioration; the responses of those in the mid-category 'concern' were much more variable; and the responses of the 'high/severe concern' category were also very variable but witnessed some of the most positive outcomes.

From personal observation, the only pupils for whom the approach was not best suited were those who lacked the capacity to concentrate for even short periods of time, as the approach requires of pupils the capacity to engage with the activities. The other set of pupils who did not respond were those who were not convinced that it could be of value to them and/or lacked a sense of self-efficacy (not believing that they could change).

## What are the variables that were felt to affect pupil outcome most?

The variables that affected outcome have been explored to a large extent within this text, but it is of value to summarise them:

### Relating to the operation of the Support Group

- the establishment of mutually respectful and trusting relationships between Support Group Leader and pupils and the climate established within the group – pupils having a sense of belonging and affirmation

- the group dynamic – the extent to which the group is able to pull together as a team and the personalities of the individuals within the group

- the key role of an adult who has faith in the child and perseveres with the child, being aware that effecting change takes time

- the scaffolding of the learning to enable the child to reach his/her full potential, the Support Group Leader acting as a mediator in the child's learning

- the need to press the child beyond what he/she understands and is comfortable with through gentle probing and the development of critical thinking skills (what Perkins would describe as 'Socratic Questioning')

- the need to challenge limiting aspirations and to open and widen horizons, helping pupils to understand the value of learning and education

### Relating to the pupil

- the extent to which the pupil is able to internalise the values of the group

- realisation in the child of the need for change and a desire to wish to improve, arising from the development of intra- and inter-personal intelligence and empathy

- the child having faith in his/her capacity to improve

- the extent to which the child is able to take responsibility for his/her behaviour

- the development of a sense of agency within the child such that he/she has the confidence to put into practice, in a range of contexts and situations, what has been learned within the groups

**The wider school context**

- the importance of context in understanding the variability in pupil response

- the recognition of the important role of the classroom teacher in either fostering or hindering pupil progress

- the need to ensure that class teachers are informed and understand the principles by which the Support Group Initiative operates

- the need for teachers to be aware of the potentially damaging effects of labelling and stereotyping to be balanced against the need to take pre-emptive action

- the need for high quality leadership, communication and staff development for all staff, including auxiliary staff

- the need to examine the relationship between SEBD and learning difficulties within the school and to build an inclusive ethos in which it is understood that pupils with SEBD are deserving of and entitled to support

- the need to ensure that there is a whole-school approach and that the initiative is fed into development planning and the timetabling arrangements for the school

- the need to understand the importance of culture in the effective management of change and to build capacity such that the approach is sustainable

**Beyond the school context**

- the need to develop an understanding of the complex factors that militate against effective learning, particularly in schools 'on the edge' (MacBeath et al., 2007), focusing in particular upon teacher expectations of pupil achievement

- the need for parental involvement and support, and partnership working between school and home and, when required, the involvement of wider agencies

## The wider implications of Support Group work

It should be evident from the range of evidence presented within this chapter and throughout the book that Support Groups can play a very valuable role in addressing the major imperatives in education across the UK and beyond. The challenges facing many countries are of a similar nature: the challenges of creating societies in which people behave with consideration, respect and courtesy towards each other; of bringing up young people such that they value themselves and others and can make a meaningful, valuable and valued contribution towards society and have an understanding both of their rights and their responsibilities; of creating an inclusive society in which young people do not feel alienated but have a sense of belonging; of enabling young people to fulfil their potential and develop their full range of talents and abilities.

The UK Government specifically advocates the use of small-group work and the Scottish Executive has invested in setting up Behaviour Units attached to Scottish schools. Yet, there is a lack of clarity (and very little guidance given) as to what should be happening within these settings, leaving teachers and school managers floundering in the dark about their roles, resulting in very mixed experiences for the children placed within them. In addition, the difficulties faced by schools in managing the behaviour of the most disturbed young people come to the fore. Such pupils may not respond to approaches such as 'Assertive Discipline' (Canter and Canter, 1992), nor are they likely to be able to cope with the demands placed upon them within mainstream classes without intensive support. 'Sin bins' are not the answer. They provide a short-term solution but are likely to lead, in the long term, to even greater alienation of pupils.

Within the Scottish context, Support Group work has the potential to make a significant contribution to a wide range of initiatives: *A Curriculum for Excellence* (SEED, 2004a); *Happy, Safe and Achieving Their Potential* (SEED 2005); the National Priorities and, in particular, inclusion and equality, creating a framework for learning, and values and citizenship; 'Excellent, Ambitious Schools'; 'Better Behaviour – Better Learning' and 'Additional Support for Learning'. Likewise, in the UK as a whole, it has a significant role to play in respect of the five key principles of *Every Child Matters* (DfES, 2004a); providing a more specialised addition to the SEAL programme and addressing the attendance and behaviour strands of the National Strategy (DfES, 2006b). It is a natural follow-on to Nurture Groups, which support pupils in the early years of their education.

**Summary**

This chapter has synthesised, analysed and evaluated a range of evidence in order to address the research questions that were initially posed and to capture the experience of all stakeholders related to the Support Group Initiative. Many positive outcomes were observed for pupils and their families but also for teaching staff within the school. It was generally felt that the approach had promoted an inclusive ethos within the school. The chapter identifies a range of variables that are likely to affect pupil outcome and concludes by examining the ways in which Support Groups can contribute towards a range of national imperatives relating to pupil support, emotional literacy, school discipline and attendance, attainment and achievement, inclusion, and values and citizenship.

# Notes

## Chapter 2

1   The long-term target was inspired by the New Haven Program as described by Goleman (1996: 276).

## Chapter 3

1   **Social capital:**   The concept of social capital is related to issues of social justice and equity. It is concerned with the quality and nature of networks that form between people which can advantage or disadvantage them. It underlies many of the government's policies on social inclusion. A clear description of social capital is provided in MacBeath et al. (2007: pp. 42–46).

2   **Theory of mind:**   The concept of theory of mind has been very influential in helping to explain the processes through which children gain a sense of their own identities and of their discreteness from others. It is not a scientific concept but is described by Astington (1994) as *belief/desire* or *folk psychology.*

3   **Means of conducting research:**   The research study was carried out using a variety of means, including questionnaires, interviews and analysis of documents and statistical data, drawing from the accounts of pupils, their parents, Support Group (SG) Leaders, Pastoral Care teachers, senior management and class teachers. All research tools were piloted as per normal practice and guidance was issued (verbally and in writing) to SG Leaders regarding the conduct of them. Normal ethical procedures were adhered to. Interviews were scribed rather than recorded and were authenticated either by the interviewer reading over the responses to the interviewee or by providing a written transcript of the interview. Interviews were conducted by the author, by Stuart Hall (SCRE) and by SG Leaders who received training to support them in this process. The study is being undertaken as a PhD at Glasgow University. For further details, contact the author at joan.mowat@strath.ac.uk.

4   **Tests of statistical significance:**   Tests of significance (in this case, derived from chi-squared tests) are a means of establishing the extent to which events could be accounted for by chance. These measures of statistical significance are used as a means of predicting the likelihood of occurrences of a similar nature happening within a similar set of circumstances. (For a simple explanation of how to conduct chi-squared tests refer to Munn and Drever, 1996: pp. 48–53.)

## Chapter 4

1   **Metacognition**: A clear description of metacognition and how it can be applied within the classroom can be found in Kirkwood (2005: 122–127).

# Chapter 6

1   **Transcripts:** The transcripts are derived from video recordings of two Support Groups made over a six-week period using a still-camera set up in a corner of the room so that pupils would gradually acclimatise to the camera. Permission was sought of parents and pupils for this to take place and normal ethical procedures have been adhered to.

2   **Learning Community:** The concept of a Learning Community has been gaining momentum in a range of professional contexts and is associated with building capacity and a sense of community within an organisation. In this chapter, however, the concept is discussed within the context of social constructivist teaching, 'Teaching for Understanding' being a manifestation of such.

## Chapter 1

Mowat, J. (1997) *Promoting Positive Behaviour*, SCRE (www.scre.ac.uk/scot-research/mowatprom)

## Chapter 3

Astington, J.W. (1994) *The Child's Discovery of the Mind*, London: Fontana Press
Brewer, S. (2001) *A Child's World: A Unique Insight into How Children Think*, London: Headline Book Publishing
Gardner, H. (1999) *Intelligence Reframed: Multiple Intelligences for the 21st Century*, New York: Basic Books
Goleman, D. (1996) *Emotional Intelligence: Why It Can Matter More Than IQ*, London: Bloomsbury
Perkins, D. and Blythe, T. (1994) 'Putting understanding up front', *Educational Leadership*, Vol. 51, no. 5, Alexandria, VA: ASCD. pp. 4–7

## Chapter 4

Blythe, T. & Associates (1998) *The Teaching for Understanding Guide*, San Francisco: Jossey–Bass
Dweck, C.S. (2006) *Mindset: The New Psychology of Success*, New York: Random Mouse.
Kelly, P. (2005) *Using Thinking Skills in the Primary Classroom*, London: Paul Chapman Publishing
Kirkwood, M. (2005) *Learning to Think: Thinking to Learn*, Paisley: Hodder Gibson
McGuinness, C. (2006) 'Building thinking skills in thinking classrooms', in *Teaching and Learning Research Briefing, no. 18*, London: TLRP
McLean, A. (2003) *The Motivated School*, London: Paul Chapman Publishing
Perkins, D. (1992) *Smart Schools: Better Thinking and Learning for Every Child*, New York: The Free Press
Smith, I. (various dates) Series of *Occasional Papers* (nos. 1, 2, 4, 5, 6 & 7), Glasgow Caledonian University: Learning Unlimited

## Chapter 5

Hamill, P. and Clark, K. (2005) *Additional Support Needs*, Paisley: Hodder Gibson (Scottish context)
Munn, P., Lloyd, G. and Cullen, M.A. (2000) *Alternatives to Exclusion from School*, London: Paul Chapman Publishing
Riley, K.A. and Rustique-Forrester, E. (2002) *Working with Disaffected Students*, London: Paul Chapman Publishing

## Chapter 8

Boyd, B. (2005) *CPD: Improving Professional Practice*, Paisley: Hodder Gibson (Scottish context)
Fullan, M. (2003) *Change Forces with a Vengeance*, New York: Routledge Falmer
MacBeath, J. and McGlynn, A. (2002) *Self-Evaluation: What's In It for Schools?*, London: Routledge Falmer

# REFERENCES

Allan, J. (2004) 'Working together to support inclusion', *Education in the North*, no. 12 (2004–2005)

Astington, J.W. (1994) *The Child's Discovery of the Mind*, London: Fontana Press

Audit Scotland/HMIE (2003) *Moving to Mainstream: The Inclusion of Pupils with Special Educational Needs in Mainstream Schools*, Edinburgh: HMSO

Blythe, T. and Associates (1998) *The Teaching for Understanding Guide*, San Francisco: Jossey-Bass

Brewer, S. (2001) *A Child's World: A Unique Insight into How Children Think*, London: Headline Book Publishing

Canter, L. and Canter, M. (1992) *Lee Canter's Assertive Discipline: Positive Behaviour Management for Today's Classroom*, Los Angeles, CA: Lee Canter & Associates

Claxton, G. (1998) *Hare Brain Tortoise Mind: Why Intelligence Increases When You Think Less*, London: Fourth Estate

Covey, S.R. (2004) *The 7 Habits of Highly Effective People: Powerful Lessons in Personal Change*, London: Simon and Schuster

DES (1978) *Special Educational Needs*. The Warnock Report, London: HMSO

DfES (2004a) *Every Child Matters: Change for Children in Schools*, London: Department for Education and Skills

DfES (2004b) *Summary of the Children Act 2004*, London: Department for Education and Skills

DfES (2005a) *Social and Emotional Aspects of Learning [SEAL] … improving behaviour … improving learning*. Ref. No: DfES0110-2005G, London: Department for Education and Skills

DfES (2005b) *A New Relationship with Schools: Improving Performance through School Evaluation*, London: DfES/OFSTED

DfES (2006a) *Inclusion: Does It Matter Where Pupils Are Taught?*, London: DfES/OFSTED

DfES (2006b) *The Standards Site: Behaviour and Attendance Guide*. www.standards.dfes.gov.uk/secondary/keystage3/issues/behaviour (accessed May *2007*)

Dweck, C.S. (2002) 'Motivational processes affecting learning', in Pollard, A. (ed.), *Readings for Reflective Teaching*, London: Continuum. pp. 118–120

DWP (2004) *Opportunity for All*, London: Department for Work and Persions

Dweck, C.S. and Elliot, E.S. (1983) 'Achievement motivation', in Hetherington, E.M. (ed.), *Socialization, Personality and Social Development*. Vol. IV of Mussen, P.H. (ed.), *Handbook of Child Psychology*, New York: Wiley. pp. 643–692

Entwistle, N. (1987) *Research on Motivation to Learn*, Edinburgh: SCRE

Everard, K.B. and Morris, G. (1996) *Effective School Management* (3rd edn), London: Paul Chapman Publishing

Fullan, M. (2003) *Change Forces with a Vengeance*, New York: Routledge Falmer

Gardner, H. (1993a) *Frames of Mind: The Theory of Multiple Intelligences* (2nd edn), London: Fontana Press

Gardner, H. (1993b) 'Educating for understanding', *The American School Board Journal*, no. 20, pp. 21–25

Gardner, H. (1995) *The Unschooled Mind: How Children Learn and How Schools Should Teach*, New York: Basic Books

Gardner, H. (1999) *Intelligence Reframed: Multiple Intelligences for the 21st Century*, New York: Basic Books

Gardner, H. (2000) Foreword to Armstrong, T. (2000) *Multiple Intelligences in the Classroom*, Alexandria, VA: ASCD

Gladwell, M. (2000) *The Tipping Point*, Boston, MA: Little, Brown and Company

*Glasgow Herald* (2006) 'Crime committed by young girls doubles', 8 June

Goleman, D. (1996) *Emotional Intelligence: Why It Can Matter More than IQ*, London: Bloomsbury

GTCS (2005) *Discipline in Scottish Schools: A Survey of Teachers' Views*, Edinburgh: General Teaching Council for Scotland

Hamill, P., Boyd, B. and Grieve, A. (2002) *Inclusion: Principles into Practice: Development of an Integrated Support System for Young People (SEBD) in North Ayrshire*, Glasgow: University of Strathclyde

HMIE (2002a) *Count Us In: Achieving Inclusion in Scottish Schools*, Edinburgh: HMSO

HMIE (2002b) *How Good is our School [HGIOS]* (rev. edn), Edinburgh: HMSO

HMIE (2006a) *Missing Out: A Report on Children at Risk of Missing Out on Educational Opportunities*, Edinburgh: HMSO

HMIE (2006b) *How Good is our School: The Journey to Excellence*, Edinburgh: HMSO

House of Commons Education and Skills Committee (2006) *Special Educational Needs*, Vol. 1, London: The Stationery Office

Kendall, S., Cullen, M.A., White, R. and Kinder, K. (2001) *The Delivery of the Curriculum to Disengaged Young People in Scotland*, Slough: NFER

Khon, A. (1999) *Punished by Rewards*, New York: Houghton Mifflin

Kinder, K., Kendall, S. and Howarth, A. (2000) 'Disaffection talks' (Conference Paper given at Inclusive and Supportive Education Congress in Glasgow)

Kinder, K., Wakefield, A. and Wilking, A. (1996) *Talking Back: Pupil Views on Disaffection*, Slough: NFER

Kirkwood, M. (2005) *Learning to Think and Thinking to Learn*, Paisley: Hodder Gibson

Lawrence, D. (2002) *What Is Self-Esteem?*, in Pollard, A. (ed.), *Readings for Reflective Teaching*, London: Continuum. pp. 102–104

Lawson, H., Parker, M. and Sikes, P. (2005) 'Understandings of inclusion: The perceptions of teachers and teaching assistants', (Conference Paper given at Nfer Council of Members Meeting, London, 4 October 2000)

MacBeath, J. and McGlynn, A. (2002) *Self-evaluation: What's In It For Schools?*, London: Routledge Falmer

MacBeath, J., Galton, M., Steward, S., MacBeath, A. and Page, C. (2006) *The Costs of Inclusion*, Cambridge: University of Cambridge

MacBeath, J., Gray, J., Cullen, J., Frost, D., Steward, S. and Swaffield, S. (2007) *Schools on the Edge: Responding to Challenging Circumstances*, London: Paul Chapman Publishing

MacGilchrist, B., Myers, K. and Reed, J. (1997) *The Intelligent School*, London: Paul Chapman Publishing

McCluskey, G. (2005) 'What does discipline mean in secondary schools now?', *SER*, Vol. 37, no. 2. pp. 163–174

McGuinness, C. (2006) 'Building thinking skills in thinking classrooms', in *Teaching and Learning Research Briefing, no. 18*, London: TLRP

McLean, A. (2003) *The Motivated School*, London: Paul Chapman Publishing

Mosley, J. (1998) *Quality Circle Time in the Primary Classroom: Your Essential Guide to Enhancing Self-esteem, Self-discipline and Positive Relationships*, London: LDA

Mowat, J. (1997) *Promoting Positive Behaviour*, SCRE (www.scre.ac.uk/scot-research/mowatprom)

Munn, P. and Drever, P. (1996) *Using Questionnaires in Small-Scale Research: A Teacher's Guide*, Edinburgh: SCRE

Munn, P., Johnstone, M. and Sharp, S. (2004) *Discipline in Scottish Schools: A Comparative Survey Over Time of Teachers' and Headteachers' Perceptions*, Edinburgh: University of Edinburgh

Munn, P., Lloyd, G. and Cullen, M.A. (2000) *Alternatives to Exclusion from School*, London: Paul Chapman Publishing

Nuthall, G. (2002) 'Social constructivist teaching and the shaping of students' knowledge and thinking', in Brophy, V. (ed.), *Social Constructivist Teaching: Affordances and Constraints*, Ch. 1, Greenwood, CT: JAI. pp. 43–79

OFSTED (2005) Every Child Matters: The framework for the Inspection of Children's Services. Available at www.ofsted.gov.uk/publications/2433

Perkins, D. (1992) *Smart Schools: Better Thinking and Learning for Every Child*, New York: The Free Press

Perkins, D. (1993) 'Teaching for Understanding', *American Educator (Journal of the American Federation of Teachers)*, Vol. 7, no. 3. pp. 28–35

Perkins, D. (1998) 'Understanding understanding' and 'The Teaching for Understanding Framework', in Blythe, T. & Associates, *The Teaching for Understanding Guide*, San Francisco: Jossey–Bass. pp. 9–24

Perkins, D. and Blythe, T. (1994) 'Putting understanding up front', *Educational Leadership*, Vol. 51, no. 5, Alexandria, VA: ASCD. pp. 4–7

Perkins, D. and Salomon, G. (2001) 'Teaching for transfer', in Costa, A.L. (ed.), *Developing Minds: A Resource Book for Teaching Thinking*, Alexandria, VA: ASCD. pp. 370–378

Perrone, V. (1997) 'Why do we need a pedagogy of understanding', in Wiske, M.S. (ed.), *Teaching for Understanding: Linking Research with Practice*, San Francisco: Jossey–Bass. pp. 13–38

Pirrie, A., Head, G. and Brna, P. (2006) *Mainstreaming Pupils with Special Educational Needs: An Evaluation*, Edinburgh: HMSO

Riley, K.A. and Rustique-Forrester, E. (2002) *Working with Disaffected Students*, London: Paul Chapman Publishing

SED (1977) *The Pack Report*, Edinburgh: HMSO

SEED (2000a) *The National Priorities in School Education: A Framework for Improvement*, Edinburgh: HMSO

SEED (2000b) *The Standards in Scotland's Schools etc. Act 2000*, Edinburgh: HMSO

SEED (2001a) *Alternatives to School Exclusion*, Edinburgh: HMSO

SEED (2001b) *Better Behaviour – Better Learning*, Edinburgh: HMSO

SEED (2004a) *A Curriculum for Excellence*, Edinburgh: HMSO

SEED (2004b) *The Additional Support for Learning Act*, Edinburgh: HMSO

SEED (2004c) *Support in Schools: The Views of Harder to Reach Pupils*, Edinburgh: HMSO

SEED (2004d) *Connect: Report on Implementation of 'Better Behaviour – Better Learning, 2004'*, Edinburgh: HMSO

SEED (2005) *Happy, Safe and Achieving Their Potential: A Standard of Support for Children and Young People in Scottish Schools*, Edinburgh: HMSO

Social Exclusion Task Force (2006) *Reaching Out: An Action Plan on Social Exclusion*, London: Cabinet Office

Swartz, R.J. and Parks, S. (1994) *Infusing the Teaching of Critical and Creative Thinking into Content Instruction: A Lesson Design Handbook for the Elementary Grades*, Pacific Grove, CA: Critical Thinking Books and Software

United Nations (1989) *The United Nations Convention on the Rights of the Child*

UNESCO (1994) *The Salamanca Statement and Framework for Action on Special Needs Education*

Vygotsky, L. (1978) 'Mind in society: The development of higher psychological processes', in Pollard, A. (ed.) (2002) *Readings for Reflective Teaching*, London: Continuum. pp. 112–113

Warnock, M. (2005) 'Special Educational Needs: a new look', in *Impact*, no. 11 (Philosophy of Education Society of Great Britain)

Wenger, E., McDermott, R. and Snyder, W. (2002) *Cultivating Communities of Practice*, Boston, MA: Harvard Business School Press

Wilkin, A., Moor, H., Murfield, J., Johnson, F. and Kinder, K. (2006) *Behaviour in Scottish Schools*, Insight Paper no. 34, Edinburgh: HMSO